LOYOLA KIDS

Book of Heroes

Amy Welborn

Other Loyola Kids Books

Loyola Kids Book of Saints
by Amy Welborn

Loyola Kids Book of Everyday Prayers
by Catherine Odell
and Margaret Savitskas

Stories of Catholic heroes and saints throughout history

LOYOLA KIDS

Book *of* Heroes

Amy Welborn

LOYOLAPRESS.
A JESUIT MINISTRY
Chicago

LOYOLA PRESS.
A JESUIT MINISTRY

3441 N. Ashland Avenue
Chicago, Illinois 60657
(800) 621-1008
www.loyolapress.com

Cover and Interior Design: Judine O'Shea
Cover and Interior Illustrations: Vitali Konstantinov

Library of Congress Cataloguing in Publication
Welborn, Amy.
Loyola kids book of heroes / Amy Welborn.
p. cm.
Summary: Introduces the lives of Christian saints and others who have heroically followed the teachings of Jesus Christ and demonstrated the seven cardinal virtues.
ISBN-13: 978-0-8294-1584-1
ISBN-10: 0-8294-1584-X
1. Cardinal virtues—Juvenile literature. 2. Christian saints—Juvenile literature. 3. Catholics—History—Juvenile literature. 4. Catholic children—Religious life—Juvenile literature. [1. Virtues. 2. Saints. 3. Catholics. 4. Christian life.] I. Title: Kids book of heroes. II. Title.
BV4645.W45 2003
282'.092'2--dc22

2003012625

Printed in the United States of America
21 22 23 24 25 26 27 28 29 30 Bang 21 20 19 18 17 16 15 14 13 12

CONTENTS

IV. *Temperance*

V. *Prudence*

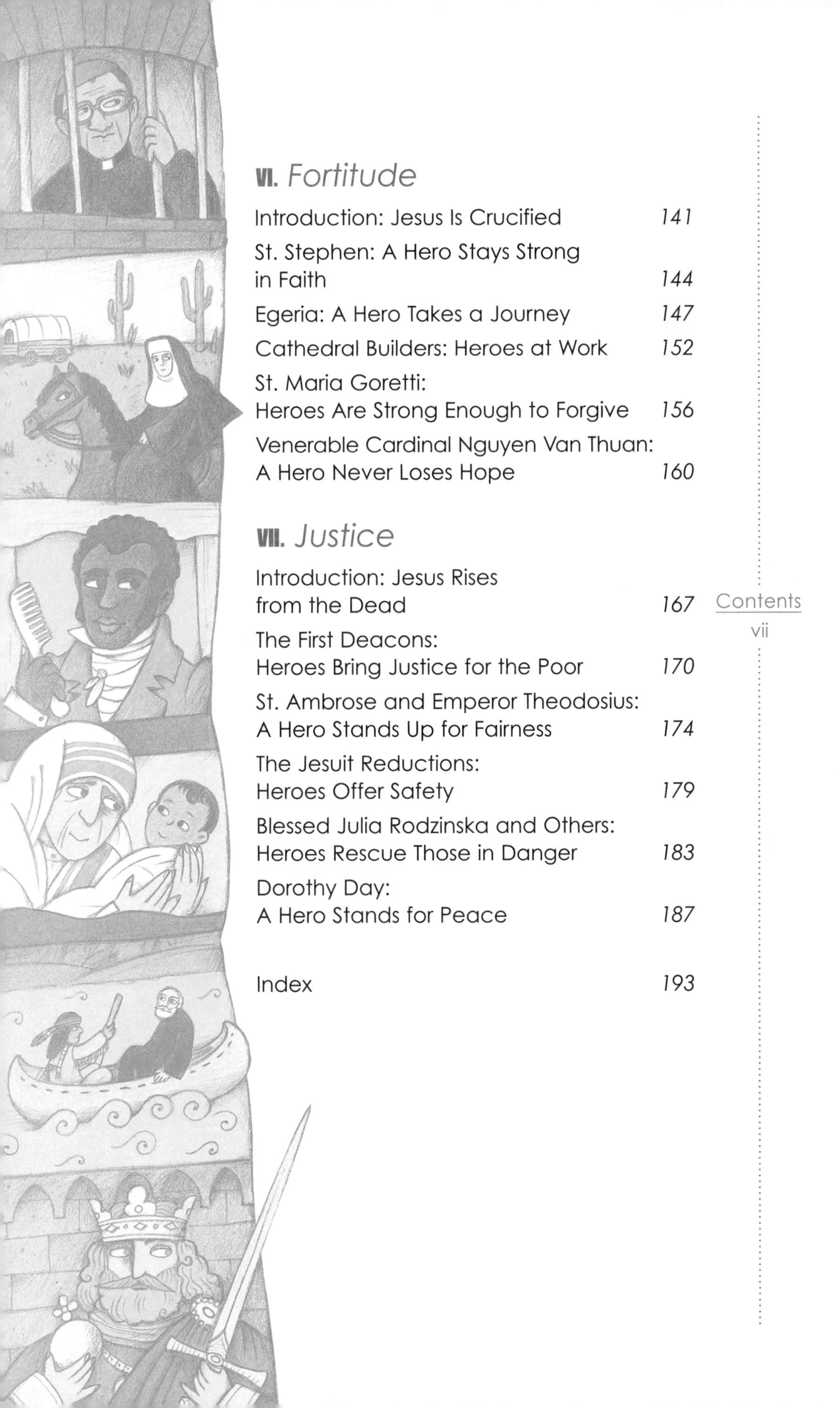

VI. *Fortitude*

VII. *Justice*

Who's Your Hero?

If you're like most kids, you probably have at least one. Your hero might be an athlete or a singer—someone who has used his or her talents in ways that you hope to when you get older. Your hero might be a brave firefighter or police officer. Or your hero just might be your own mom or dad.

Good for you!

It's really important to have heroes. Heroes help us learn how to live. They help us see what's possible. They give us something to work for as we grow up.

But if you think about it, as great as those kinds of heroes are, there just might be something missing. After all, what's the most important part of your life? What do you have that is going to last your whole life, no matter where you are or what you're doing? What is it that's even going to last after you die?

Your friendship with God. That's right, your faith.

Sure, life is filled with all kinds of exciting chances and possibilities. God wants you to jump into life and experience them! He wants you to enjoy life and make the most of it. It's great to work for those goals.

But without a friendship with God that is above, beyond, and underneath all that everyday busyness, our life can seem kind of empty at the end of the day. Without friendship with God, we can also be tempted to use all those wonderful gifts to hurt ourselves and others, rather than help.

So if we're friends with God, we just might need another kind of hero to add to all the rest. We need some heroes who are close friends with God and who put him first.

Since Jesus rose from the dead and Christianity began, there have been thousands of heroes like that. You probably have heard the names of some of them. Some of the more famous heroes of faith have been recognized by the church as being especially close to God; we call these people saints.

But whether their names start with Saint, Blessed, Venerable, or just Mrs. or Mr., all of these heroes have something in common: They all lived lives of virtue, centered on friendship with God.

Virtue is, quite simply, goodness. There are many ways to be good—being patient, kind, and honest are just a few. Over time, Christianity settled on seven of the most important virtues. These types of goodness really show what loving God is all about.

First there are three spiritual virtues:

Faith When we have faith, God is our best friend. He comes first, no matter what, and we believe what he says is true.

Hope When we have hope, we trust that God's promises are true, and we don't let ourselves be discouraged.

Charity *Charity* is another word for love. When we have charity, we love as God loves, seeing every person we meet as God's child and treating him or her that way.

Four more virtues are called *moral* virtues because they are the beginnings of all of our good actions.

Temperance When we practice the virtue of temperance, we treat the things of this world properly. We are grateful for things as gifts of God, but we don't put them in the place of God.

Prudence When we practice the virtue of prudence, we make wise decisions. We apply God's love and wisdom to the choices we make.

Fortitude When we practice the virtue of fortitude, we're strong. We trust that God is with us and that God will help us do the right thing, no matter what.

Justice When we practice the virtue of justice, we treat every person as a child of God. We remember that God created the world to be a good, happy place where everyone is treated fairly.

None of these virtues are given to us when we're born, ready to use like a present. The seeds are there, but it's up to us to make the virtues real in our lives. God gives us the grace to live in faith, hope, and charity, but we have to cooperate with him to make it happen.

The people in this book are heroes who brought these seven virtues to life in our world. They're not superheroes, though—they are just like you and me—human beings who were good at some things and bad at others. These heroes had problems and joys. Some were adults when they did the things we admire them for; others were kids about your age. But being strong or working for justice didn't come easily to any of them. They had to dig deep within and let God help them, just like you. Their goodness and holiness didn't happen overnight.

These virtues can be hard to live by, but it's like anything else: We have to start small. After all, you can probably do big multiplication problems now, but could you always? Could you always hit a ball as far as you can now? Could you always play the violin so well? No, you couldn't.

You started out small, with the little things. You learned your numbers, then how to add and subtract, then your multiplication tables, and then even harder math. You played T-ball first, then used a pitching machine, and now you're the pitcher yourself! When you first picked up that violin, all you could do was bang on the strings with your bow, and it didn't sound so great—but listen to you now!

It's the same way with the life of faith and virtue. Sure, being strong enough to start hospitals for the poor is pretty amazing—but this strength started somewhere small—perhaps even in childhood, sharing food with a friend, collecting pennies for the poor, and just looking at the world with compassion and love.

These heroes teach us many things. They teach us that no matter who we are, we can be friends with God. They teach us about the happiness and joy that come into our lives when we put our friendship with God first. And they teach us that with God's help, any of us can change the world. Any of us can be heroes, too!

Faith

I am the way, and the truth,
and the life.

John 14:6

Jesus Is Born

Did you ever have an invisible friend when you were little? Lots of kids do, so don't be ashamed to admit it. It's really just a part of growing up.

These days, your friends aren't invisible, are they? They're walking and talking all around you—at school, in your neighborhood, and on your sports teams. It only takes a second for you to remember their names and what their faces look like. You can even use your memory and imagination to see the way they run or hear them tell a really bad joke.

Being friends would be hard if you couldn't see, hear, or even touch these boys and girls. It wouldn't be impossible, but it would be a pretty big challenge.

Faith is really nothing more than letting God be your best friend, but that can be hard sometimes. We can't see or hear God the same way we can see and hear our best friend walking on earth. Being friends with God seems to be different than that. How can we start? How can we know where to meet God and start our friendship of faith with him?

Lucky for us, God understands everything, including this problem. Here's how he solved it: He became one of us.

Many hundreds of years ago, a woman named Mary and a man named Joseph held a bundled-up baby in their arms. Huddled in a cave that served as a home for animals somewhere around Bethlehem in southern Judea, they counted fingers and toes, kissed a damp forehead, and thanked God for a healthy baby, born safely.

Mary and Joseph probably thought of other things, too, the night that baby Jesus was born. They thought about all they'd been told about him—before he was even born.

They remembered how Jesus had been created by God in a very special way inside Mary, without Joseph's help. They remembered their long, hard journey from Nazareth in the north to

Bethlehem in the south, where the government had called them to be counted and taxed.

And they remembered that this birth was full of surprises. Listening to angels and watching the shepherds come to pray and honor their baby Jesus, they understood that he was a gift. He was a gift like all babies are gifts, but even more so. All babies hold promise and hope, but baby Jesus held an even greater, more important promise than any other baby ever born.

An angel had told Mary about this promise when he told her she was miraculously carrying this child. The angel Gabriel had said that Mary's baby would be called "Emmanuel," which means "God with us."

Talk about a great gift! Can you imagine any greater gift than that?

In Jesus, God gave the world the most wonderful gift it had ever known—himself. This baby wasn't just a gift for his own family, he was a gift for the whole world. The all-powerful, all-loving God who'd created the world was wrapped up in a blanket, being fed by his mother, and peacefully going to sleep.

Sometimes, because God is so great and we are so small, we have a hard time understanding God. We're sort of like a baby trying to figure out the big grown-up world. It's very hard for us with our little baby brain to understand what's going on. In the same way, we are babies in relation to God. We have a hard time figuring out what God is like. Some people have a very hard time knowing that God loves them and that they have a wonderful reason for living.

God knows this, and because he wants us to know and love him, he gave us a great gift to make it easier: Jesus, his Son. God with us. All those big questions we have about God are answered in him. First, the baby Jesus is helpless—what love God must have for us to come among us so weak and dependent! And when we watch the baby grow into a man and see him heal, forgive, and love, we can see that God is all about healing, forgiving, and loving, too.

When we see this same man dying on a cross even though he had done no wrong, we once again feel in the deepest part of our hearts what God's love really means—that he will do anything for us.

Finally, when the man appears to his friends, who thought he was gone forever, we see how far the gift of Jesus will take us: to eternal life with him—and that means forever.

All babies give us gifts, of hope, of love, of cuteness. The baby Jesus gives us a special gift that no other baby ever gave: the gift of faith. For when we watch this baby, we know who God is and what a good friend he is to us. Knowing this makes it easier for the virtue of faith to grow in our lives.

Faith is believing that God loves you. It's being best friends with God and letting him lead you to happiness. It's putting God absolutely first, all the time, no matter what, knowing that you can live forever in happiness with God.

Jesus, God born as a baby, is a gift to you and me and the whole world. He was given so that we can see and hear God talking to us in ways that we can understand, in ways that make it easier to be friends with God.

Let's see what happens when we open our arms and accept the gift!

John the Baptist

A Hero Prepares the Way

There are times when your faith can definitely make you stand out in a crowd. You might be wearing a cross or religious medal around your neck. Maybe everyone noticed when you paused and said a little prayer before lunch or a test. You didn't mind, though. Your best friend, God, is there for you all the time. It doesn't bother you to let others know that you're there for him, too.

Oh, and speaking of standing out in a crowd—was that you, dressed in animal skins and eating locusts?

No, no. I was wrong about that. It wasn't you. Or me. It must have been John the Baptist, then.

When we have faith, we don't just believe in ideas about God. We love him as our Father and our best friend. We're ready and willing to do what he asks because we trust him. God asks his friends to do different things. Sometimes we're called to love quietly, and sometimes with a bit more noise. And sometimes some of us are even called to be prophets.

You can read about prophets in the Old Testament. You may have heard of Isaiah, Jeremiah, Amos, Joel, and Ezekiel, who were prophets to the people of Israel. But there's also an important prophet in the New Testament. His name was John the Baptist.

The lives of prophets are often marked by startling, strange events, and John the Baptist's life was no different. For you see, John the Baptist's parents, Elizabeth and Zechariah, were both rather old. In fact, they were as old as your grandparents—or maybe even your great-grandparents! They were way too old to be having babies of their own.

Elizabeth and Zechariah thought so, too, although they had been praying for a child for many years. One day when Zechariah, a Jewish priest, was praying in the holiest part of the temple, an angel came to him and told him some shocking news: Not only would he and Elizabeth have a child, but this very special child would prepare the people of Israel for the coming of the Lord. Of course, Zechariah was a little startled by this and found it hard to believe. So the angel gave Zechariah a sign: He struck him mute—unable to speak.

And mute he remained for many months. He couldn't say a word to welcome Elizabeth's pregnant cousin Mary for a visit. He couldn't run out and announce the miraculous news of his son's birth. But soon after, God made sure that everyone heard what Zechariah had to say.

The day had come to name the baby. All of the family insisted that the baby should be named after his father. Elizabeth told them that no, his name was to be John, something they didn't understand and didn't believe until one more amazing thing happened.

Zechariah, for the first time in months, started talking! He told them that yes, the baby's name was to be John. So, of course, everyone had to wonder what this amazing baby was all about. God had already done great things in his life. What could be next?

Thirty years later, they found out, and as we read the Gospels, we find out, too. The next time we see John, he is all grown up and living, not with his parents, not in a village or a town, but out in the desert, near the Jordan River.

And yes, he's wearing those scratchy, hairy animal skins and living on something you may like to eat, honey, and something else you probably wouldn't eat in a million years—locusts, which are bugs similar to grasshoppers.

More important than his clothes or his diet, however, were John's words. He lived in the desert preaching and teaching an important message, given to him by God because, of course, he was a prophet of God.

John told the people who traveled out to the desert that they should listen to him. He said that it was time for them to ask God's forgiveness for their sins and to change their lives because someone very special was coming. The Messiah that the Jewish people had been awaiting for centuries had finally been sent by God and would come among them soon. He baptized people as a sign that they were ready to change their lives to welcome God's messiah.

One day, just as John promised, the Messiah did come. Jesus came to the river Jordan and told John to baptize him. Now, this startled John because he knew that Jesus had never sinned and so didn't need to be washed of his sins. But Jesus insisted that John go ahead and baptize him, as a sign to the people of his humanity. It turned out to be a sign of something else as well, for when John poured the water on Jesus, a voice spoke from heaven: "You are my beloved Son, with you I am well pleased."

But John's work wasn't done, even after that. He continued to preach and baptize, telling everyone about Jesus. He also talked about the wrongdoing of religious and political leaders, and this is what finally got him into terrible trouble.

Herod Antipas was the governor of the area in which John lived. John had criticized Herod for marrying Herodias, his own brother's wife. This made the whole family angry, and John was imprisoned in order to silence him.

One evening, Herodias's daughter, who was named Salome, danced at a party Herod was hosting. Herod was so delighted with Salome's talent that he told her to ask him for anything, and he would give it to her. Salome rushed to her mother and asked her what she should say. Herodias saw this as her chance to get rid of a very irritating part of her life. She told Salome to ask for the head of John the Baptist.

Herod wasn't crazy about this idea, because even though he, too, was criticized by John, he still found John an interesting speaker and, as the Gospel of Mark tells us, "he liked to listen to him" (Mark 6:20). But, of course, Herod couldn't be shamed in front of his guests by breaking the promise he'd made to Salome, so he ordered what Herodias and Salome had requested. John was executed, his head was presented to the women on a platter, and the voice of this prophet and truth-teller was silenced.

But not forever, right? For when you read the Gospels today, you can still hear the voice of John the Baptist calling you to make good choices and to look for Jesus.

He may have looked and acted rather strangely, but that's the way it can be when you answer God in faith. Faith means looking to God for guidance and ignoring what the world tells you is right or correct or fashionable. It means listening to God, just as John did, and following the path he calls you to. Sometimes that's easy, especially if you're hanging out with others who share your beliefs, but sometimes it can be hard.

John could have said no to God. Any of us can. God doesn't force anyone to do anything. He especially doesn't force us to be friends with him in faith. But John said yes. He said yes to friendship with God, no matter where it took him. Right now, two thousand years later, God is offering his love and friendship to you and me.

What's our answer?

Early Christian Martyrs

Heroes Are Faithful Friends

Friends are friends no matter what, right?

Well, you sure hope so. You hope that your friends won't let you down when you need them most. You depend on them to not reveal your secrets or make fun of you in a mean way.

Friendships can feel really strong and easy to keep in good times. But the test of a friendship happens when, for some reason, we're tempted to betray our friends. If we can stick out the temptation, we know that our friendship is real.

It's good to remember that faith is a friendship—a close, trusting friendship with God. We're loved, supported, and helped

by God all day long. We tell him our troubles and our joys. You and God go through each day together, and he will be with you for the rest of your life. That's a friendship. That's faith.

Sometimes you might be tempted to betray that friendship, just a little bit. You might be embarrassed to admit that you go to church or pray. You might think it wouldn't be so bad to hurt someone else's feelings—just this one time. You might stop reading the Bible or praying at night because you've got other things to do. You're not the first to feel that way, you know. And you won't be the last.

In fact, Christians have been tempted to betray their friendships with God ever since the beginning, in both big and small ways. And just like any friendship, every time we resist that temptation and stay faithful to that friendship, our faith grows stronger.

For the first three hundred years of Christianity, the followers of Jesus were under great pressure to betray their friendships with him. They lived in what was known as the Roman Empire, which extended from northern Africa all the way up to England at that time. For almost the entire period from A.D. 100 to 313, it was illegal to be a Christian in most of the Roman Empire.

That's right, illegal—against the law. In our country, you can go to court and go to jail for things like stealing and killing. In the Roman Empire, you would go to jail for those things, too. But you could also be punished by the law if you were friends with Jesus.

How? Every person in the Roman Empire, no matter what their religion, was supposed to honor the Roman emperor as a god. If they would do that—once a year burn a little incense in front of a statue and say, "Caesar is god!"—they were okay and could go on home and mind their own business for another year.

But, of course, Christians refused to do this. They knew there was only one God, and to say anything or anyone else was a god would be a betrayal of their friendship with God. When they stood true and when they refused to honor false gods or the emperor as a god, the Christians got into trouble. Big trouble.

They were put in jail—dark, terrible dungeons. They were sent into exile to desolate islands where they were forced to work in mines. And worst of all, if they were really stubborn and still wouldn't deny their friendship with Jesus, they were put to death.

The leaders of the Roman Empire did this because they really wanted to discourage others from following Christianity. They also wanted to provide entertainment for the people of the empire. So when they executed Christians, they often did it in public, in the middle of huge crowds gathered in arenas. It was, believe it or not, like a big show.

There are many stories of the deaths of Christians that have come down to us over the centuries. These Christians who died for their faith were—and still are—called "martyrs," a word that means "witnesses." They're called witnesses because that's exactly what they were doing through their deaths: witnessing to their love for God and their friendship with him—their faith. Some of the more well-known stories of martyrs from those early years include the following:

St. Lucy, St. Agnes, St. Agatha, and St. Cecilia were all young women—perhaps in their early teens—who all suffered terribly for their faith at different times. The stories that have come down to us say that St. Lucy lost her eyes during her torture, St. Agnes was beheaded, St. Agatha was placed on hot coals, and St. Cecilia was suffocated and then beheaded.

St. Timothy and St. Maura were married only twenty days when Timothy, who was in charge of the sacred books of his Christian community, was ordered to turn them over. He refused, and his wife, Maura, was brought to the prison to try to convince him to give in. She wouldn't cooperate, so both husband and wife were nailed to a wall of the prison, and, so tradition tells us, it took them nine days to die.

St. Marcellinus was a priest who was imprisoned during the last major Roman persecution, around A.D. 304. While in prison before his execution, he convinced many of the love of Jesus, including his own jailer.

There are hundreds—thousands—of other martyrs from these years who endured the most terrible pain. But the strange thing is, the stories that come down to us about their deaths, even those few stories recorded by the Romans who killed them, tell us that most of these women, men, and children who were killed for their faith died with peaceful hearts, sometimes even singing hymns as they were burned or dragged by animals in front of the cheering crowds. Their friendship with God was very, very deep.

Over the past two thousand years, many Christians have decided to die rather than betray their friendship with Jesus. Even today, Christians still suffer martyrdom in some countries. You will read about some of them in other chapters in this book.

All of these brave people may speak different languages and wear different clothes, but they all have something important in common: They are best friends with Jesus, and they can't imagine turning their backs on him, even if it means suffering.

You probably know how they feel—you can't imagine turning your back on your own friends. When you're tempted to, you probably just have to imagine how rotten you'd feel if you did, and that's enough to set you straight.

Well, when you're tempted to betray your faith—your friendship with God—remember that feeling. And remember the martyrs of early Christianity. Just imagine if they had all chosen to deny their friendship with God instead of staying true.

Would anyone else have bothered to even look into friendship with Jesus if the Christians had betrayed him? Would it have seemed worth living for, if it wasn't worth dying for?

Medieval Mystery Plays

Heroes Make the Bible Come to Life

What do you enjoy doing with your friends? Probably a lot of things. You probably like to talk, shop, watch movies, or play games.

Once in a while, you might even get bigger ideas. You might spend a whole day building a snow fort or making cookies. You might take more than a day—maybe a week—organizing a neighborhood soccer tournament or talent show or even making a

movie. You're not doing this because anyone told you to but because you wanted to. It's fun to work on things like that with a friend. You get to know each other better, and when it's all over, you can look at what you've done—whether it's just a pile of cookies or a homemade movie like *Attack of the Mutant Teachers*—and you'll see something solid and real that celebrates your great, kind-of-weird friendship.

When we're friends with God, we can't help but want to celebrate that, too. We can do it in simple, everyday ways by taking time to talk to God during the day and listen to his voice in our hearts. But we can get busy, too, when it comes to our faith—our friendship with God—and we can make a big deal of it. We can write a poem or make a picture. We can help with a big project at our church. We might even have fun. That's okay, you know.

There was a time in Christian history when people absolutely loved to make a big deal of their friendship with God. During the Middle Ages (around 1000 to 1500), faith inspired Christians to build great churches, paint beautiful pictures, and write gorgeous music.

And then there were the plays.

Yes, you heard me right—the plays. Have you been to a theater to see a play? Well, these plays were quite similar, except they weren't performed in theaters. They were mostly presented outside, in towns and villages all around Europe. These are special kinds of plays called miracle plays and mystery plays.

Anywhere you went in Europe during the Middle Ages, you would find, at one time of the year or another, groups of people dressing up, making sets, and performing plays about God's friendship. Quite often, the whole town would get involved, and the result would be a huge play with many parts that would take several days to perform.

The medieval mystery plays were about every nook and cranny of faith. Some plays made the Our Father or the Creed come to life. Characters would act out the main points of the prayer, using stories from the Bible. In miracle plays, Mary or another saint would appear to help someone in danger.

Other plays were about particular stories in the Bible. The creation and Noah's ark stories were popular. Saints' lives were popular, too. Around Christmas, towns liked to present the story of Jesus' birth. And around Easter, most large towns presented a play dramatizing Jesus' death and resurrection—these were called passion plays. Some of these plays could be very long. One version of a passion play presented in France lasted forty days! In one production in Germany in 1437, a priest playing Jesus on the cross almost died, but he was taken down just in time.

You can see that these plays were taken very, very seriously!

There were no theaters during this time, and it really wasn't appropriate to perform these plays in churches, so most of the performances took place outside. Sometimes the sets were stationary—with the different scenes in a play set up in a row or in a circle—and the audience would have to walk to the various stages to see the entire play.

Other times, the sets were constructed on wagons. Quite often, the presentation of plays was part of a festival or town fair related to a religious feast, and a parade would be part of the festivities. Horses or oxen would pull the decorated stages through the town as a way to get the townspeople excited about the plays!

The plays were written in verse and performed in the language of the people (rather than in Latin, which was the language used by the church). There was great seriousness in the plays, because these were serious subjects, but there were also often humor and clownishness. There was one more thing, something that all the people who watched and put on the plays loved: the special effects.

It may not seem like much to us today, but if you try to imagine living in a time before television and movies, you might be able to feel some of the interest that people had in these effects. Audiences marveled as clouds would part to reveal God sitting on his throne. They would be amazed as angels actually flew through the air. Firecrackers were used to show lightning and large sheets of copper to make sounds like thunder. Large sheets of fabric would look like the waves of the ocean, and some of the more elaborate plays managed to use real water on their stages. Fires full of hot, glowing coals showed the audiences what hell might be like.

The miracle and mystery plays of the Middle Ages were wonderful, creative spectacles. But they were something else, too. The people who came to see them were there because they wanted to understand God better and know more about him. They wanted to see the stories of God's friends from the past. They also wanted to have a little fun—and, after all, isn't that an important part of friendship, too?

St. Albert the Great and Others

Heroes Study God's Creation

When you like another person, it's natural to want to know what makes that person tick.

Why does your friend like to play soccer so much? What's with the obsession with horses? He moved around a lot before he finally settled in your town, down the street from your house. What was it like to live in so many different places? Does she think the new music teacher is as kooky as you do?

Real friendship is about caring, loving, and knowing. Not knowing too much, now—let's not get nosy here—but knowing

so you can appreciate more and more how great your friend is and what makes him or her unique.

Faith is really a friendship with God, and the deeper your faith is, the more you're going to want to know about God. So loving God just might lead you to read the Bible more and to pay more attention at Mass. You're not alone. Throughout history, people who were close friends with God, people who had deep faith, were moved by that faith to explore what God is all about. Many of them shared their discoveries with the rest of us through their books, songs, prayers, and art—and through their scientific explorations.

This might surprise you, because you might not be used to thinking about science as a way to know more about God. But for hundreds of years, Christians thought that way all the time. Smart, curious men and women looked at the wonderful world God had made and got excited about it. They got excited not just because the universe is so fascinating (which it is!), but because they knew that when they studied that universe, they might just come to appreciate and love their friend God more, as well.

For a long time after the beginnings of Christianity, no one thought much about science at all—they were too busy surviving. They were trying to survive Roman persecution, first of all, and then after that ended, they were trying to survive the very difficult years we call the Dark Ages—from about A.D. 500 to 900. Life in Europe during the Dark Ages was quite harsh. The Roman Empire had collapsed and nothing had arisen to take its place to make life safe and secure for people. The only thing holding life together was the Christian church.

By the 1200s, light was starting to shine again. For many reasons, people felt safer, towns were growing, and people could start learning and exploring the world around them again. Because they didn't have to just worry about simply surviving any longer, they had time to stop, think, and create. They started building beautiful cathedrals. They began studying at universities. And they started thinking about science again.

A fellow named Albert was a part of this. Today we call him by a couple of other names: we call him Albert the Great, and more important, we call him St. Albert: He's the patron saint of scientists!

St. Albert the Great lived from around 1200 to 1280. He was a member of the Dominican religious order. Albert's family didn't think much of his choice to join the Dominican order at first, for they were a wealthy family and the Dominicans were dedicated to a life of poverty. But Albert won that battle and spent the rest of his life being amazingly busy. He was a leader in his order, he was an excellent preacher, and he was even a bishop for a couple of years! He was a good teacher, too. Do you know how we know this? Because his most famous student was the brilliant St. Thomas Aquinas, whose ideas have been very important to Catholics for hundreds of years.

As part of his role as a bishop and leader in the church, Albert had to travel all around Europe, quite often on foot. In his travels, he observed the land, plants, and animals, and he traveled so much, he got the nickname the Bishop of the Boots. All along, Albert was exploring scientific ideas. He wrote about the plants he saw in his travels and about chemistry. He wrote about the human body. He loved geography and made maps of the mountain ranges of Europe.

Albert also demonstrated that the world was round, not flat—you may think that Christopher Columbus was the first person to think that the world was round, but it's not true. People had thought it was round for hundreds of years before Columbus made his first voyage in 1492, and St. Albert was one of those who helped show that it was true.

Albert was also interested in building things. There's a story that he built a little air-powered mechanical man that played a flute!

St. Albert the Great, of course, wasn't the only great Catholic scientist inspired by his faith to explore God's world. Nicolaus Copernicus (1473 to 1543) was a Polish priest who developed the idea that the earth revolved around the sun, rather than the other way around. Gregor Mendel (1822 to 1884) was a monk who used the peas and other plants he grew in his monastery garden to discover how parents pass on physical traits to children—what we now call genetics.

And do you know who runs the oldest astronomical observatory in the world? The Vatican—the home office of our church—does, that's who! It was founded in 1891 and still exists today, with telescopes and research sites not only in Italy, but also in Arizona!

Friendship can lead you down all kinds of wonderful paths, can't it? Your care for another person can expand your world and help you appreciate how interesting and beautiful life is.

Friendship with God, faith, can do the same thing. When we love God a whole lot, we want to know more and more about him. Studying the things he's made—from the peas growing out of the ground to the stars circling in the sky—is a wonderful way to do just that.

Sister Blandina Segale and Others

Heroes Work in Faith

During the hot days of summer, just about the best place to be is the swimming pool, a lake, or the ocean. Anywhere you can find cool water to jump in, right?

Speaking of jumping—do you remember when you first learned to dive into the water? Do you remember the first time you went off a high diving board?

If you're like most kids, that first time—and maybe even the time after that—was just a little bit scary. Maybe you would have just liked to walk away and try another time instead. And maybe

what finally got you up and off and into the water wasn't just your own determination—did a friend have something to do with it? It's not just that you didn't want to be embarrassed in front of your friend (well . . . maybe that was part of it). Your friend's presence gave you the little boost of courage you needed to take that adventurous step into the air and down into the water.

Now that wasn't too bad, was it?

Friendship can give us the strength to do a lot of things we might not try if we were alone. Sometimes, when we've got a friend there to support us, it's easier to do something new, work a little harder, or even reach out to help another person in need.

If our human friends can give us so much encouragement, just think what we can do when we're friends with God!

The story of our church is made up of stories of men, women, and children who have done great things. Many times, we hear these stories of bravery and sacrifice and we think, How could they do that? How could they make it? And how could they be happy in a life that looks so hard? The answer is pretty simple. God was their best friend, and with him at their side, they could climb up whatever diving board was in front of them with confidence and trust.

In the 1800s, millions of people traveled from Europe to settle in growing cities on the East Coast of America. Then they moved into new territories in the West, in search of fresh land and opportunity.

For much of that time, there were only the roughest roads, no trains, and of course, no cars or airplanes. Whole families traveled in coaches and wagons through forests, across plains, and over mountains. And very often, close behind, came little groups of women, all dressed in black or blue robes, following the same path but for different reasons. They weren't looking for farmland or ranch land for their families. They were Catholic nuns looking for people in need. Why? Because their best friend, Jesus, had called them to, and they said yes.

When you think of the Old West, you probably think mostly of cowboys, Native Americans, and cattle drives. From the very beginning, though, Catholic sisters were also a part of life in the West, often in very surprising ways.

The sisters who went out West usually worked in two areas: education and medicine. Catholic nuns started schools in every corner of the country; by 1900, there were more than four thousand schools run by Catholic nuns in the United States.

Catholic nuns also ran hospitals and medical clinics. By 1900, they ran almost three hundred hospitals. About one-fifth of the nurses who helped soldiers during the Civil War (1861 to 1865) were Catholic nuns, and they were very much loved by the injured soldiers they served. One sister who worked in a military hospital wrote in a letter, "They often said it was the sisters who cured them, and not the doctors."

The work of these brave sisters wasn't easy. They were women traveling on their own, without any protection, in times and areas where the law could be hard to find. Most were from Europe, and English wasn't exactly their first language. They would be invited to a town to set up a school or hospital and arrive to find nothing ready for them. Much of the time, the sisters did their own hard physical labor in either fixing up old buildings for use or just constructing new ones.

Worst of all, there was the sad fact that in those days, more people than you could imagine were very prejudiced against Catholics. Catholic nuns, with their long habits, were quite visible, tempting targets for that prejudice. The letters these sisters wrote back home to Europe are filled with stories of bad treatment, from being pelted with stones as they walked along a street, to having their convents and schools burned to the ground. And these things happened not just in the lawless West, but in towns across the United States in the 1800s, from Massachusetts to Texas.

But these things never stopped the sisters. The stories of the Catholic nuns who brought faith, education, and medicine to the West are stories of bravery, love, and friendship with God and God's people. And these stories can be very exciting also.

You could probably make a movie about the life of Sister Blandina Segale. When she was twenty-two, she traveled alone out West and spent the next two decades working in Colorado and New Mexico. She built hospitals and schools from nothing, confronted angry lynch mobs, and even met Billy the Kid!

Billy the Kid was, in case you don't know, one of the most notorious outlaws in the Old West. He wasn't a character in a tall tale—he was a real person who led a real gang of thieves and murderers, bringing great fear to communities he threatened. One of his gang members became seriously injured in the town where Sister Blandina lived. He had been left lying helpless in a hut on the edge of town. No one dared visit him, so of course, Sister Blandina had to go.

For two months she visited him twice a day, bringing him food, cleaning his wounds, sharing the love of Jesus with him through her actions. One day the man told her that his gang leader was coming, and with a purpose: Billy the Kid was going to scalp all four doctors in town because none of them had been willing to treat his friend.

So, as you might expect, with her friend Jesus giving her strength, Sister Blandina showed up at the little run-down shack at the same time Billy the Kid and four of his gang members did. Billy wasn't angry or mean—this time. He thanked her for caring for his friend and said that if there was anything he could do in return, let him know.

Of course there was—he could turn away from his plan to scalp those doctors. And that is exactly what he did, because of the bravery of Sister Blandina.

The Catholic sisters who brought the love of Jesus to the Wild West faced challenges and adventures they could never have imagined back in Europe or in the cities of the East Coast. But because of their deep faith, their close friendship with Jesus, they found the courage and strength to face it all—from sickness and hard physical work to dangerous criminals.

In faith and friendship, they took Jesus' hand—and they jumped!

Hope

Rejoice in hope.

Romans 12:12

Jesus Teaches

Did you see your math homework yet? Did you see those thirty long-division problems? And the spelling words you have to write five times each and the definitions you have to look up?

Don't you ever wonder just what all of it is for and why you have to spend so much time on these little picky things that seem so pointless? But believe it or not, they aren't pointless. These picky little things give us small skills that we can use to build big talents, or they give us a chance to practice good habits in small ways. Hope is the virtue that helps us see this. Hope is the virtue that helps us see beyond the present to the good that's waiting in the future.

You know that studying fifth-grade science isn't going to be your life's work, but being there and doing your best is going to help you somehow—you hope. Trying to be a better person might hurt sometimes, but you do it anyway because the good, hard choices you make today will help you be a better person forever—you hope.

Hope helps us see beyond the boring, and even sometimes painful, necessities of life so that we can realize what some of the picky little things are really for: living a happy and joyful life, just as God wants us to.

Sounds great, right? But how can we do this unless we know what God's promises are? Are we just supposed to figure them out for ourselves? Fortunately, no. There's no guesswork about God's promises, because God has told us all about them.

When Jesus, God-made-human, walked the earth, he did many things. He worked miracles. He reached out to the poor and the sick. And he taught.

Wherever Jesus traveled, he taught. He taught at dinner parties. He taught on top of hills and standing in a boat near a lakeshore. He taught in the middle of the night to people who were too scared to come see him during the day. He taught women, men, and children. He taught the poor and he taught powerful leaders. He taught using the Scriptures; and he taught very, very often by using special stories called parables.

Jesus taught because God wanted people to have hope. Without hearing the Good News, it would be easy to live without hope. What's the point of doing good? How can I ever make up for the wrongs I've done? I'm not as good looking, talented, or smart as some other kids in my class. Why am I here anyway? What's going to happen to me after I die?

Just imagine how you would answer those questions if you didn't have a clue about the Good News, if you'd never heard what Jesus had to say about them. Pretty sad, huh? Maybe a little empty? Maybe without much hope?

Now think of the promises Jesus made and how they give us hope.

We're all tempted to misuse our time. The choice between studying for your social-studies test and watching television can be hard—unless you can see beyond the moment and have hope in the good the hard work will bring. Thinking about the parable Jesus told about the man who built his house on sand, only to see it washed away in a storm, might help (see Matthew 7:24–27).

When we do something wrong, we can be tempted to feel that there's no way we can be forgiven and no way we can start over. We can lose hope—unless we remember one of the many parables Jesus told about forgiveness: the story about the shepherd who rejoiced when he found his lost sheep (see Luke 15:1–7) or the story of the prodigal son who returned to his forgiving father (Luke 15:11–32), just to name a few.

When we're wondering if it's worth it to be kind, we could think about the parable of the good Samaritan. Jesus promises that helping is always the best choice, and we can have hope in that.

There's no doubt that God made us and wants us to be happy. But that can be tough sometimes, and it can be really hard to see how life fits together, especially when you're a kid.

That's why the virtue called hope is so important. When we have hope, we're trusting in God's promise that if we follow him, happiness will be ours. We may not be able to see it right now, but

God has promised that it's true. Through the stories and wisdom of Jesus, we know what these promises are, promises made by God so that we can have hope. And you do remember who God is, don't you?

He's your best friend.

That's a pretty good reason to trust in his promises, don't you think?

Pentecost

Heroes on Fire with Hope

Hope can be a lot like your homework folder at 7:30 in the morning: hard to find when you need it most. Even if everyone around you has told you to calm down and stop worrying, it's not so easy, is it?

If you've ever lived through a really sad loss, you know how true this is. No matter what it is—a death, a divorce, or even just a move away from the old neighborhood to a new one—you feel like you'll never be the same, and you'll be sad forever. Eventually you realize that what your family and friends have been telling

you is true. In time, you will get over the shock and the deep pain. After a while, the world seems like a little brighter place.

Yes, sure—you know this. But it's still hard to feel it. It's still hard to have hope.

Since you know this, you can probably imagine what Jesus' friends felt after he died, rose, and ascended into heaven. Of course, they had seen amazing things—the most amazing thing in the world, in fact: their teacher and friend Jesus risen from the dead. They'd heard him speak time and time again of the new life with him that awaited them and all people who believed. They'd even heard him say that they wouldn't be alone even after he ascended into heaven. The Spirit would come, he said, the Spirit that would bring them comfort and help.

So yes, they'd heard all of this, and they believed it. But still . . .

The apostles were only human, you know. They loved Jesus with their whole hearts. They believed him. He'd told them to go out to the whole world and share the good news of God's love and forgiveness. They had every intention of doing just that, really. Jesus had told them it would be hard but that it would be all right in the end, that the Spirit would come . . .

But where was it?

A few weeks after Jesus' ascension into heaven, the apostles were still waiting. What's more, they were waiting, it seems, in fear, and you really can't blame them. After all, they were still staying in Jerusalem, the city where their leader Jesus had been publicly executed as a criminal. Do you think they were excited about going out into that same city and preaching the same message that got Jesus arrested and killed?

It's true. Jesus had told them over and over again to have hope. They'd even seen his words proven true with their own eyes, as Jesus, once dead, walked among them alive. But they just couldn't seem to get themselves out there into those crowds. They were still afraid. They couldn't respond to Jesus' promises in hope.

And so they waited, stayed, and prayed. Eventually, a few weeks after Jesus' ascension into heaven, the Jewish feast of Pentecost rolled around. This feast, usually called Shavuot today, is a time when the Jewish people celebrate God giving the Law to

Moses on Mt. Sinai. As they did on other important feasts like Passover, many Jews liked to travel to Jerusalem, the city that was the center of their religion, to celebrate Pentecost. People do the same thing today. Many Catholics like to be in Rome to celebrate Christmas or Easter, for example.

So while the city was filling up with Jewish people from all around the world, the apostles were in a closed, locked upper-floor room of a house, thinking about the joyful promises of Jesus, but probably thinking just as much about the sad and scary crucifixion of Jesus. How could they hope?

Praying in that room, weeks after Jesus had physically left the earth, the apostles got their answer. First, it came in a sound of rushing wind that filled the house. Then it came in fire. Not a fire that was going to harm them, but, as the Bible says, "tongues" of fire that came to rest over each of their heads.

You can bet the apostles knew exactly what this meant. Their Jewish ancestors had experienced the power of God in both wind and fire many times—remember the burning bush? the pillar of fire that led the Israelites through the desert? the wind that swept over the waters at Creation?

The wind and the flames filled the room, and the apostles knew that Jesus had sent the Holy Spirit. He had kept his promise. God had come to them with hope.

God's Spirit gives us all kinds of gifts. It gives us strength and courage. It gives us wisdom. When you hear what the apostles did on Pentecost, you can see how true this is.

For right then and there, those apostles, who had been so frightened before, rushed right out into the busy city of Jerusalem and started telling the crowds about Jesus.

You remember, of course, that the people in Jerusalem had come from many different countries and spoke all sorts of languages. The strangest thing happened, though, when the apostles started preaching: Each person heard the words of the apostles in his or her own language! It was such an amazing scene, and the apostles were so excited that some in the crowd even thought they had been drinking too much wine!

Peter, the leader of the apostles, set them straight. "It's only nine o'clock in the morning!" he reminded them as he started to talk about Jesus, telling the crowds that Jesus was the long-promised Messiah who had been raised from the dead. His words were so powerful, the Bible tells us, that on that day, three thousand people were baptized as new followers of Jesus!

That's quite a change, isn't it? The apostles could barely stand the thought of leaving their safe closed room in Jerusalem. They wanted to do the right thing. They wanted to go out and tell the world the wonderful good news about Jesus. But something held them back—until the Spirit came to give them hope!

It's good news of hope, there for you the same way it was for the apostles at Pentecost. When you're afraid and lonely and can hardly find any reason to smile, you can think about those apostles and do just what they did. You probably won't find yourself in the middle of a wind or see any flames, but if you close your eyes and sincerely ask Jesus to send his Spirit to give you hope, you know he will.

Why? Because he promised to, that's why!

St. Paul

A Hero Changes and Finds Hope

Sometimes change is great. Starting a new school year with different teachers is usually pretty exciting. Redecorating your room can be a blast. Even something simple like cutting your hair in a new style is fun.

But sometimes change seems nothing but awful and scary. Moving to a new town, enduring a divorce or a death are changes that all of us would rather avoid if we could.

Any change gives us new reasons to grow in the virtue of hope. After all, it's easy to trust in God when everything's the same as it always was. But when life shifts, we can sometimes be tempted to lose hope and to believe that God isn't big enough to help us no matter what. When we continue to hope despite the way life changes, it means that our friendship with God is getting deeper.

Enough about us. Let's talk about a man who went through an amazing change—from a persecutor of Christians to being one of Jesus' best friends.

His name was Paul.

Actually, when we first meet him in the book of the Bible called the Acts of the Apostles, his name was Saul.

As a young man, Saul lived in Jerusalem, studying the law—the rules that God gave the Jewish people to live by. Like many others, he was disturbed by the followers of Jesus. He was bothered when they said that Jesus was the Messiah, the savior Israel had been waiting for. This man Jesus, after all, had been executed as a criminal! How could anyone say he was the Messiah? Saul was so disturbed, in fact, that he stood by as a witness to the stoning death of the first Christian martyr, Stephen. Soon after that, Saul began persecuting other Christians, pulling those accused of following Jesus out of their houses and sending them to prison.

If you had taken a poll back then, you would definitely not find this Saul anywhere near the top of the list of "Most Likely to Become a Christian."

But you know how life can change, don't you?

Life changed for Saul when he was on his way from Jerusalem to a city called Damascus, about one hundred miles away. He was, of course, out to arrest more Christians.

Not so fast, Saul. Not so fast.

> Now as he was going along and approaching Damascus, suddenly a light from heaven flashed around him. He fell to the ground and heard a voice saying to him, "Saul, Saul, why do you persecute me?" He asked, "Who are you, Lord?" The reply came, "I am Jesus, whom you are persecuting. But get up and enter the

> city, and you will be told what you are to do." The men who were traveling with him stood speechless because they heard the voice but saw no one. Saul got up from the ground, and though his eyes were open, he could see nothing; so they led him by the hand and brought him into Damascus. (Acts 9:3–8)

When Saul finally arrived in Damascus, blind and confused, a Christian man named Ananias came to visit him. Ananias, by the way, had not heard about Saul through the paper or even town gossip. He'd been told about Saul in a vision from God, and when Ananias arrived, he told Saul that he had been sent there by Jesus.

Suddenly Saul's heart could see that Jesus was working in his life. What seemed like scales fell from Saul's eyes, and he could see. Saul was baptized, and his life changed forever.

But Saul didn't become a whole new person from top to bottom, of course. Even though he'd accepted this huge change in his life, and even let himself be known as Paul as a symbol of that change, he was, in some ways, the same man he'd always been—and that's exactly what God wanted, we can almost be sure.

God wanted Paul to know him and serve him, but he didn't need Paul to become a totally different person to do that. Paul was strong and brilliant and passionate. He was overflowing with courage and vision. God didn't want Paul to lose any of those qualities. He wanted these qualities to be used for good, though, not harm.

So Paul spent the rest of his life—about fifteen years—absolutely devoted to telling every person he could about Jesus. He traveled endlessly. He was shipwrecked, imprisoned, and beaten. He put up with the distrust of his fellow Christians, who found it hard to believe that he was genuine, and not a spy.

You know St. Paul not only from the story about the big changes in his life, but also from something else you hear almost every Sunday in church: the letters, or epistles, he wrote to the Christians in the towns he visited. These letters make up about half of the New Testament, and they're full of advice, practical wisdom, and words that let us know how strong St. Paul's faith was.

A man named Saul placed his hope in a certain idea of what God wanted. A big change shook him up and challenged him to think in a new way. He could have lost hope, sitting there in the dark in a strange town far away from friends and family. But instead, Saul listened to what Jesus had told him on the road, and he found a new, deeper, stronger hope in God's love.

Change is always going to be a part of your life. Always. Sometimes you'll find it easy to accept change, and some changes will be hard. Hope means trusting that God is a part of your life, no matter how it changes. Hope means getting through changes and, instead of complaining, trusting that God knows what he's doing. Hope is turning to God and asking, "Okay—what do you want me to do now?"

St. Patrick and St. Columba

Heroes Bring Hope into Darkness

It was only one game, you know.

It was one soccer game in which your team was tied with the other team. Despite all your best efforts, your opponents got the ball in your team's net with ten seconds to go. Did we mention that this game was for the city championship? Did we mention that you were the goalie?

Did we mention that all of this happened on the day you learned you made a D on a social-studies test, and, as if life couldn't get any more rotten, a couple of hours after your team had lost the game, you came down with the flu?

Sometimes when so much of life seems so dreadful, it's hard to figure out what's good about it. But we have to, you know. Your dad still makes great pancakes. Your mom still hugs you. Your best friend is still your best friend. And God still loves you—a lot.

No matter how bad life can seem, God is still with us, and that means we can still find hope no matter what. It's true for us, and it's true for the whole church, too.

Believe it or not, the church goes through bad times, too. In fact, the life of the church is a lot like your life—it's usually a mix of good and bad, sad and happy, and goodness with a bit of sin thrown in, sadly enough. There are times, though, in which things seem darker than ever. Many hundreds of years ago, the church endured one such hard time, a time that today we call, naturally enough, the Dark Ages.

The Dark Ages was a period in the history of Europe from about A.D. 500 to about 1000 in which life was very hard for everyone, little scientific progress was made, and most people lived in small villages, just barely getting by. There was hardly any growth in learning or art or thinking anywhere in Europe. (That's why we call it "dark," in case you hadn't figured it out yet.) It was pretty sad everywhere—everywhere except Ireland, that is.

You know about Ireland, I'm sure. It's a small island nation just west of England and Scotland. You've probably heard of St. Patrick, who brought Christianity to the people of Ireland in the fifth century and who convinced many of them in an amazingly short time to turn from the false ideas of worshipping spirits and nature to worshipping the one true God. The story you may not have heard of is the one that tells who came after Patrick to continue his work of spreading the light of hope in a dark time.

When St. Patrick worked to spread Christianity in Ireland, he did it mostly by starting monasteries: places where men or women could live, work, and study God's word. Monasteries quickly became important centers of education and religious life in Ireland and other countries.

The monks and nuns who lived in these monasteries had to work hard to live, just as everyone did in those days. Remember, this was more than a thousand years ago, and unless you were part of a king's family, you probably had to provide for yourself all of your own needs, from clothing to food. Monks and nuns were no different. Their monasteries were busy centers of farming, weaving, crafts, and of course, learning. They were really the only places where learning was going on!

During these years, many great men and women spent their lives sharing the Good News in Ireland and even beyond. One of the most well known (besides Patrick, of course!) was St. Columba.

St. Columba was born to noble parents, but very early he decided to leave that life behind and become a priest. He became very busy, founding monasteries and teaching and preaching in Ireland, until he got involved in the most interesting—and sad—situation.

Columba, like all of the Irish Christians, loved the books that taught him about Jesus. A teacher of his owned a quite beautiful and complete book of the Gospels. (Remember at this time, there were no printing presses and no bookstores. All books were hand-copied—imagine how valuable they were because of that!)

Columba asked his teacher if he could copy the book for his own use. The teacher said no, but Columba so badly wanted a copy of the Gospels for himself that he snuck down at night to copy it. His teacher discovered what he was doing and demanded that he be given the copy. The argument got so bad that they had to go before the king, who ruled in the teacher's favor. This infuriated Columba, who, even though he was a monk, went to his own family and encouraged them to make war against the king. It is said that three thousand people died in the fighting.

When Columba saw what terrible things his stubbornness had brought about, he was stricken with guilt (thank goodness!) and decided he must leave his beloved home of Ireland and go to other lands. The penance he gave himself was this: He would spend the rest of his life working to bring as many souls to God as he had caused to be lost in the senseless battle. So he, along with some of his fellow monks, got on a boat and set out, landing on an island called Iona (in the sea between Ireland and Scotland) where they started—you guessed it—a monastery. For the rest of his life, Columba used Iona as his home base to bring the hope of Christianity to the people of Scotland, a land where he came to be as loved as he was in Ireland.

Columba did, indeed, bring many souls into friendship with Jesus. He also had a few interesting adventures. Have you heard of the Loch Ness monster? This mysterious creature is said to live in a big, dark, mysterious lake, Loch Ness, in Scotland ("loch" is "lake" in the ancient Scottish language). Well, St. Columba is the first person recorded in history to have seen the Loch Ness monster. The story goes that one of his monks was swimming in the lake to get a boat for Columba. The slinky, slimy monster broke the surface of the water and roared. St. Columba ordered it, "Think not to go further, nor touch thee that man. Quick, go back!" And it did!

In Europe, the years we call the Dark Ages were difficult, indeed. There were hardly any schools, and people young and old struggled just to survive. But as hard as it was to survive, at the very same time, there was light shining in one tiny corner of the land. Up in Ireland, songs were being sung, books were being written, and people were accepting the Good News with joy. In time, it was the Irish Christians who went across the sea to teach, preach, and spread the Good News and help the struggling Christians in the rest of Europe rediscover the richness of their faith.

So no matter how dark things seem, somewhere, somehow, there is hope waiting to break through, sometimes from where you least expect it. It's always been true in the church's life, and it's true in your life, too.

The world may seem to be against you, but God never is. Bad stuff happens to you, but that doesn't mean your life is just totally bad. Somewhere, somehow, there's a glimmer—like Ireland shining through the Dark Ages—that shows you God is with you, and always will be.

Hold on to that, and you won't lose hope!

St. Jane de Chantal and Others

Heroes Hope through Loss

We all have special people in our lives. We have our parents, our grandparents, our brothers and sisters, and our friends. We love them all—even the brothers and sisters! These wonderful people gave us life, help us get through the day, and help us understand how to make sense of this crazy world.

If you think of your life as a puzzle, all of these people would be pieces in that puzzle, making the picture whole and complete. What happens if one of the pieces goes missing?

You may have had this happen to you. Perhaps someone important in your life has died. Maybe there's been a divorce, and one of those people who used to be around all the time isn't around anymore. Maybe you've moved. Or they have.

Any way it's happened, losing a person's presence in your life is really hard. It shakes up the puzzle and forces you to look at the picture of your life in a new way. The challenge of loss can even lead you to question what life is all about, and even to lose hope.

So sure, hope can be hard to come by when we experience loss. But that's also when finding hope is most important. Just ask Madame Jane de Chantal. Or, if you like, St. Jane de Chantal.

Jane, who lived in France in the seventeenth century, was a beautiful, smart, and lively young woman who was blessed to marry a man she loved very much: Baron Christophe de Chantal.

Together, Jane and Christophe had six children. Only four of the children survived infancy (this was not unusual in those days before modern medicine), but sadly, only two weeks after the youngest baby, Charlotte, was born, tragedy struck the family: Christophe, the children's dad and Jane's husband, was killed in a hunting accident.

Jane, of course, was devastated. She mourned for a long time, and she worried, too. Even though the family was not poor, she still worried about her children's futures and how she would be able to give them the guidance and help they needed as they grew up. She wondered about something else, as well.

For you see, besides being smart (especially with money, fortunately), Jane had one other strong quality: She loved God passionately and felt a little urging, deep within her soul, to give her life over to him in service. But how?

In those days, if a woman wanted to dedicate her life wholly to God, that meant being a religious sister, and that meant, for the most part, joining a convent that had very strict rules about interacting with the outside world. Today, there are still convents like that, but there are also many religious sisters who work in the world, teaching, helping the poor, and working in medicine. During the time Jane lived, such a life was hardly ever allowed.

So what was Jane to do? She had lost her beloved husband. She had four young children to support. She felt pulled toward a kind of life that really had no room for her. It would have been very easy for Jane to lose hope then, wouldn't it?

Just at that moment, though, God sent someone special into Jane's life. It was a bishop—Bishop Francis de Sales of Geneva, who came to Jane's parish as a visiting preacher. Francis was wise and loving. He was devoted to helping everyone come closer to God, no matter who they were or what kind of life they led. In a time when many thought only priests, nuns, and monks could have a deep friendship with God, Francis knew better. The books that he wrote about prayer and following Jesus were for everyone.

So Francis de Sales was the perfect person to bring hope to Jane de Chantal. She thought his preaching was wonderful, and he thought she was blessed with a deep and strong faith. They became friends.

Francis helped Jane see God's will for her life more clearly. She finally understood that there was hope: she could, indeed, be faithful both to her family and to God. Here's how: She could start a whole new kind of religious order for women. The women who joined wouldn't lead a life closed up in a convent. They would live and pray together, but they would also leave their shared home to help the poor and the sick. Jane decided to call her new kind of order the Sisters of the Visitation of Holy Mary. She named the group after the Visitation—the time Mary went to visit and care for her elderly cousin Elizabeth, who was pregnant with John the Baptist.

This kind of life helped Jane express her deep desire to bring Jesus' care and love to those in need, and it also made it possible for her to take care of her family. It was the perfect solution! Her letters, many of which you can still read today, tell the story of these exciting years. Jane wrote to women who were founding houses for the Visitation Sisters (more than eighty were founded during her life). She wrote to women who asked for her help in their prayer lives. And, of course, she wrote to her children, offering them advice and guidance just like any mother does.

St. Jane de Chantal isn't the only widow to go on beyond her loss and do great things for both her family and God. St. Elizabeth Ann Seton was left with five children when her husband died in 1803, and she went on to do something pretty important—start the Catholic school system in the United States. St. Marie Guyard was widowed with one child when she was only nineteen years old. When her son was old enough to take up a trade and follow his own path, St. Marie joined the Ursuline Sisters, moved from France to the wilds of Canada, and spent the rest of her life ministering to French settlers and Native Americans. She even wrote readers and catechisms for the indigenous peoples in their own languages. St. Margaret D'Youville also lived in Canada. She was widowed at age twenty-nine with six children. She supported her family mostly through sewing, and then began to work with the very sick and poor in Quebec. She eventually ended up taking over the hospital, running it herself, and saving it from failure!

When you lose someone important, life changes; and that change is certainly sad. It can also throw your life into turmoil as you wonder, "What should I do next?" As these women who loved Jesus show us, the answer is in the virtue of hope. If you know that God has a plan for you—and he does—you can go on. And how can you figure out what that plan is? Do what all of these women did: Pray and then look—look in the eyes of the people around you who are in need. It's there that you'll find hope. And they will, too.

St. Mary Faustina Kowalska

A Hero Finds Hope in Mercy

Even the happiest, most energetic kid can feel discouraged sometimes. Doing your best on a paper and still getting a bad grade can discourage you. Asking nicely for a privilege and being turned down anyway is pretty discouraging.

Digging a little bit deeper into your heart, you might find more serious kinds of discouragement. You can sure feel discouraged and frustrated when people try to stop you from doing what

you know is right. Even more seriously, we can get to feeling awfully sad about ourselves when we do something sinful.

Is that who I am? we wonder. *How can I ever make up for this? I did this bad thing—can I ever be a good person again? Does God love me anymore?*

When others tell us we shouldn't follow our conscience, we can lose hope. We can also lose hope when we ourselves fail to follow our conscience. Don't worry. Even in the midst of that kind of discouragement, there's hope. The story of St. Mary Faustina Kowalska shows us where.

Helena Kowalska was born in Poland in 1905, the third of ten children. From very early in her life, she felt a special connection with God. When she was sixteen years old, she decided that the best way for her to live out her deep love for God was to give her life to him by becoming a nun.

You might think that everyone would have been pleased by Helena's decision—after all, what could be wrong with wanting to be a sister? Well, as it turned out, not everyone was pleased, and Helena's road to the convent was a bit longer than she ever could have imagined.

Her parents were against the idea, first of all. They loved Helena very much and knew that if she joined a convent, they would hardly ever see her again.

Second, Helena was poor. In those days, young women who wanted to join convents were expected to bring at least enough money with them to pay for their habits—the clothes they would be wearing—and perhaps more to contribute to their support. Helena didn't have anywhere close to the money she needed; so, trying not to lose hope, she decided to work to earn it.

Helena worked as a housemaid and a nanny. She did a wonderful job and was always well loved by the children she cared for. She kept asking her parents for permission to join a convent, but they kept saying no. Helena stayed focused on her prayer life, but she also began to lose hope that she'd be able to follow Jesus as she felt called to do. It all seemed impossible.

Along the way, as much as she wanted to be a nun, Helena had never stopped enjoying life as any teenager would. One evening she was attending a dance with her sister, having a wonderful time, when in the middle of the party, she started feeling strange and a little scared. In an amazing moment, what Helena saw around her changed. The room fell away, and instead of the nicely dressed, young, healthy dancers, all she saw was Jesus—injured, barely clothed, and very sad. He asked her how long it would be until she said yes—how long was he going to have to wait?

And although that vision was a little scary, it gave Helena a new sense of hope. She knew what she'd been feeling was right, and now here was Jesus, telling her that yes, he wanted her heart completely.

So right away, Helena got on a train and traveled to where Jesus had directed her: Warsaw, one of the biggest cities in Poland.

It would be hard to imagine a situation that seemed more hopeless than that: a poor young woman alone in a large, strange city, looking for a convent that would accept her—without the permission of her parents.

But Helena didn't lose hope because she knew Jesus was with her. She listened to him in her heart and, helped by a kind priest, found a place to live—again, with a family whose children she would care for. She started knocking on convent doors until she found one, the Sisters of Mercy, that agreed to accept her.

Even then, Helena's troubles weren't over. Her life in the convent wasn't easy. She was not very healthy and was unable to do much of the hard work that was asked of her. Because of that and because of her deep, mysterious prayer life, some of the other sisters in the convent grew jealous of Helena—who was now Sister Faustina (which means "blessed one")—and some of these other sisters were even cruel to her.

But again, as difficult as life got, Sister Faustina didn't lose hope, because in the midst of her difficulties, something wonderful was happening. She was becoming closer and closer friends with Jesus, and he was sharing all kinds of good news with her. The best news of all was about his mercy.

What's mercy, anyway? Mercy is just another word for God's love and God's forgiveness of our sins because of that love. Jesus spoke to Faustina about his mercy all the time, and once, he asked her to do something very strange: He asked her to have a picture painted.

It's true. Jesus told Faustina to go to an artist and ask him to paint a picture of Jesus the way Faustina saw him: standing in a white robe, one hand reaching to heaven and the other reaching to us. Two rays of light were to come from his heart: one pale and one red. The pale ray symbolizes the water of baptism, and the red, the blood of Jesus. Under the image, the artist was to write the words "Jesus, I trust in you."

It was a picture of God's mercy. Jesus knows how sin hurts us. He knows that when we sin, we feel terrible. We even feel as if God can't love us anymore and that there's no hope for us. The picture and the words underneath let us know very clearly that there is hope. Jesus is always here, ready to forgive and shower us with his love!

Well, Faustina had the picture painted, and slowly, but surely, people started coming to see it. They also started praying the prayers Faustina suggested, prayers that are all about the Divine Mercy—the special name for this idea of the love and forgiveness of God.

Of course, the attention paid to Faustina's special friendship with Jesus didn't always help the other sisters in the convent try to get along with her any better. Some of them were even more envious than others. But more of them grew to understand that Faustina wasn't making things up. She wasn't trying to show off. She was just sharing the good news that Jesus was sharing with her.

Faustina was young when she died: only thirty-three years old. She had suffered a great deal during her life. She had suffered rejection and misunderstanding. She had suffered frustration because of being discouraged by so many from following her heart. She had suffered from bad health.

You suffer discouragement, too. But when you look at the life of St. Faustina, you probably see something important: Even in the most discouraging moments, we should try not to lose hope. Why? God is everywhere and with us every moment—even the discouraging ones. If he's there, with all of his love, how can we lose hope?

Charity

And now faith, hope, and love abide, these three; and the greatest of these is love.

1 Corinthians 13:13

Jesus Works Miracles

What do you love?

Hanging out with your friends? Your dog? Playing basketball? Summer vacation?

How about pizza? Spaghetti and meatballs? Would you say that you love ice cream? Now how about your parents?

You've probably noticed that *love* is a word that gets used a lot. You might have also noticed that we use it to talk about a bunch of wildly different things. After all, loving your parents is different from loving pizza.

Now forget the pizza, the dog, and even your parents for a minute. You know by now that God is all about love. Jesus is pretty clear on the importance of love. He told his disciples (and that means us, too, by the way) that he was giving them a new commandment that would sum up all of the other ones that God had given his people through history. Jesus said this:

"Just as I have loved you, you also should love one another" (John 13:34).

But what is this "love"? Is it like loving pizza, or loving your dog, or even your best friend? Not quite, and if we watch and listen to Jesus, we can figure out what this "love" he's talking about means.

Jesus accepted everyone, even people who were rejected by everyone else. He offered God's mercy to all who asked for it, no matter what they had done. That's love.

Jesus shared God's mercy and healing with those who were suffering. That's love.

He brought sight to people who were blind. He gave speech to those who were mute. He took the paralyzed by the hand and helped them walk again. He touched the skin of lepers, and they walked away clean.

Once, in fact, the crowds around Jesus were so thick that the friends of a paralyzed man had to lower him down through a roof so he could receive Jesus' healing touch, pick up his mat, and walk away!

Jesus even brought the dead back to life. The Gospel of John tells us about the sad day when Jesus found out that his good friend Lazarus has died. He went to visit the family, and although Lazarus's sisters warned him about the smell, Jesus ordered that the tomb be opened—and then he told Lazarus to come out. And he did!

Jesus also worked other kinds of miracles that helped people. He knew that being hungry can make us suffer, too. The Gospels tell us that a couple of times Jesus felt sorry for the huge crowds that had come to listen to him and hadn't brought enough food to last through the long hours of the day. So, moved by love, he had the apostles gather what food they could, and then give it out to the crowds. As you probably remember, the meager amount of food they gathered was, miraculously, enough to feed everyone.

These weren't magic tricks, you know. Jesus wasn't doing these things to show off, either—although at the very beginning of his ministry, the devil had tempted him to do just that.

No, Jesus was working these wonderful miracles out of love. He was letting us know that God doesn't like it when we suffer. In God's kingdom, in fact, there won't be any suffering at all. When Jesus worked a miracle, he was giving us a little preview right here on earth of what God's kingdom is like.

In the Bible and in our church's tradition, we have a name for this special kind of love: We call it *charity*. Charity means loving God first, and then loving others as God loves them.

So you can see that this kind of love—charity—is a little bit different from the love that is talked about in the movies, in television shows, and in a lot of the music you might listen to. That kind of love is usually just about feelings. Charity is about a lot more.

First of all, it's about seeing. When we're best friends with God, we try to see the world as he sees it, and that means seeing it—and every person in it—through the eyes of love.

Then, it's about acting. It means listening to people and seeing their suffering, and then trying to do what you can to help. It means putting other people's needs before your own. Sometimes acting out of love gives you a warm feeling right away, but sometimes it doesn't. After all, helping out your grandmother on a Saturday afternoon may not make you as immediately happy as playing ball or going to the mall might have. Think about the kid in your class that "everyone" has decided to hate and make fun of. Choosing to treat that kid with love, dignity, and respect is probably going to hurt for a while, and maybe pretty badly.

But this isn't news to Jesus. He knows how much love costs. But he also knows something else: that when you really love, you don't care about that cost. No price is too high for love, is it?

St. Peter and St. John

Heroes Are Known by Their Love

Everyone says the new girl in class is really kind of weird.

Hardly anyone seems to like her, she sits alone at lunch, and some kids even make fun of her behind her back. All because she seems different.

Well, of course she's different. *Everyone* is different from everyone else. But, you're probably wondering, why does *this* kind of different get a girl rejected?

The reason is simple. The kids have decided to see this girl in a certain way. They made a choice.

Now, just imagine how different things might be if these kids (and you're not one of them, are you?) made a different choice. What if they decided to see this girl with the eyes of love? What if they decided to see her the way God sees her? What would happen then?

Christian love—the love we call charity—is about that kind of choice. It's about making the choice to see all people in the world as God sees them and to treat them that way.

The earliest Christians understood this. After all, remember that they were still on fire with the Holy Spirit given to them at Pentecost. The book of the Bible called the Acts of the Apostles tells us how the earliest Christians loved with the love of Jesus because they saw the world through his eyes, and they lived out that love:

> Now the whole group of those who believed were of one heart and soul, and no one claimed private ownership of any possessions, but everything they owned was held in common. . . . There was not a needy person among them, for as many as owned lands or houses sold them and brought the proceeds of what was sold. (Acts 4:32, 34)

So what made the life of these early Christians different? Well, they lived together—maybe not in the same house, but perhaps close together in the same neighborhoods. They wouldn't let any one of their new Christian family suffer from want. If someone was hungry, they were given food. If their clothes were worn-out, they helped make newer garments.

Why? Because these early Christians saw each other with the eyes of love. They looked at their neighbor and saw, not a stranger or just a person living next door, but a brother or sister in Christ. Would you let your brother or sister go hungry? Seriously, now . . . you wouldn't. Admit it.

But the earliest Christians saw non-Christians through the eyes of love, as well. Christians were known for their generosity and care for all the poor. The Acts of the Apostles also contains many stories of the apostles sharing God's love with others in the same amazing way that Jesus did: through healing.

One day, the apostles Peter and John were going to the Jewish temple in Jerusalem to pray. You see, in these early years, most Christians still considered themselves part of the Jewish faith. They thought of themselves simply as Jews who believed that the Messiah had, indeed, finally come to earth, and that the Messiah was Jesus. It wasn't until forty or fifty years after Jesus' ascension that the Jewish and Christian faiths divided.

So, Peter and John shared the Eucharist in their homes on the Lord's Day. But they also gathered with other Jews in the temple and in the synagogues to continue to pray the ancient Jewish prayers.

Arriving at the temple that day, Peter and John saw a paralyzed man lying outside the temple gate, begging. This wasn't unusual. Poor people often gathered outside the temple, hoping that people going to pray might hear God's call to care for the poor.

Peter and John looked at the beggar, and Peter said something surprising: "I have no silver or gold, but what I have I give you; in the name of Jesus Christ of Nazareth, stand up and walk" (Acts 3:6).

And he did. He got up and walked. Not only did he walk, but he leaped, jumped, and praised God. I think you can understand—you might do some running and jumping, too, if that happened to you.

At that moment, St. Peter and St. John didn't have any money to share with the paralyzed man. But they did have the eyes of love, seeing him as God sees him, with deep love and care for his pain. They could have just walked on past him and wished him well. They could have hoped that someone else would step in and be nice. They could have just tried to forget him. They could have made fun of him as they walked away.

But since God doesn't ever turn away from our suffering and doesn't ever forget us, they couldn't either. So the man walked.

Why don't you try it? The next time someone bugs you—even if it's your mom or dad—pause and take a second to imagine. Forget about what's bugging you and how you'd like to react, and imagine that other person alone with God—the God who is his or her loving father, just as he is yours. How does God see that person? What does God hope for that person? What does the virtue of charity call you to do?

Picture that girl sitting alone in the lunchroom, too. Mean kids have decided to see her one way. You don't have to join in. You can put another pair of glasses on—the ones that help you see that girl as God's child and your sister, the ones that help you see her with love.

So now what are you going to do?

St. Genevieve

A City Is Saved by a Hero's Charity

Love comes in all shapes and sizes and pops up in all kinds of places you expect, and some you don't. Love can be as quiet as a smile between classes or a good-morning hug. Love can be as loud as a family reunion or a sleepover with your best friends.

A lot of the time, sharing love is pretty easy. Living out the virtue of charity—seeing and loving others as God sees and loves us—just seems natural. We don't even have to think about it.

But sometimes, it takes courage to love. Sometimes it seems as if being friends with God—seeing others through his eyes and loving as he loves—is going to cost us. It could cost us time, money, or our pride. It might cost us a "friendship," believe it or not.

Saints are people who have faced that choice about loving, not once or twice, but over and over again in their lives. They were afraid, just like you are. They wondered if it was worth it, just like you do. And in the end, they decided that since nothing was more important to Jesus than love, nothing would be more important than love to them either.

St. Genevieve, who lived long ago in fifth-century France, faced this choice. Her choice wasn't about anything small, either—it was about the safety and health of the people of an entire city!

The city was Paris, and even more than a thousand years ago, it was the most important city in France. Genevieve had been born in a small village several miles outside of Paris. Genevieve stayed in that village until her parents died when she was about fifteen. She then traveled to Paris where she and two other young women publicly committed their lives to God.

In case you're thinking that Genevieve's life was going to stay calm and unexciting while she quietly served God in her corner of the big city, think again. These were busy, dangerous times in Paris, so it was no time for living behind a wall and minding your own business. Love brought Genevieve out into the streets of Paris, where people needed hope and courage. They were her brothers and sisters. How could she say no?

You've probably heard of a guy named Attila the Hun. He was a nasty fellow, and the Huns were a tribe known for their cruelty. In 451, the Huns threatened Paris, and the people of the city, knowing what everyone knew about the Huns, were ready to just give up.

But Genevieve—the young woman known throughout the city for her prayer and her love for the poor and hungry—wouldn't let them. She inspired the men of the city to be brave and defend themselves. She gathered the women and led them in prayer—days and weeks of prayer. It wasn't an easy time. In their fear, the people were tempted to turn against

Genevieve. Wouldn't it be easier to just give up and let the Huns take control? Wasn't Genevieve leading them to defeat and probably death?

Eventually and miraculously, the Huns turned away from Paris and headed in another direction. From that day on St. Genevieve has been celebrated as a special protector of the city of Paris.

Many years later, around 486, when Genevieve was a much older woman, she made another choice to love the people of her city. The city was being attacked (again!) by another tribe of barbarians—the Franks, this time. The Frankish army had cut off the city's food supply and were trying to starve the people into defeat.

Genevieve could have made many choices. She could have tried to find food for herself. She could have simply waited out the attack with her people. But Genevieve, moved by charity, made a different, very brave choice. She decided to try to get food for the entire city of Paris!

How? Paris is built along the banks of a great river called the Seine. This river runs through the center of Paris and out into the countryside. If you ever go to Paris, one of the things you'll probably do is take a boat ride down the Seine and see the sights of the city.

Well, in 486, Genevieve also took a boat ride down the Seine, but it wasn't to have fun. In the dead of night, Genevieve got a long boat—some say she led a group of several boats—and snuck past the Frankish troops outside the city. She traveled down the river until she came to some friendly villages, where she told the farmers of the terrible suffering that the people of Paris were enduring. The boats were filled with grain, that night and many other nights. Genevieve took the grain back to the city and distributed it to the grateful people, saving Paris once again!

St. Genevieve's life was full of love. In between the big events that made it into the history books, St. Genevieve spent her days in prayer and in helping others in small ways. But when the time came to take a risk and love in a big way, St. Genevieve kept right on loving. How could she do that?

St. Genevieve saw the people of Paris through God's eyes, as his children and her brothers and sisters. She loved them, so she didn't even have to think twice about helping them.

So when loving someone seems hard, take a minute and imagine how God sees that person and how much he loves that person and wants him or her to be happy.

You might be amazed at what happens next!

St. Meinrad, St. Edmund Campion, and Others

Heroes Love Their Enemies

Thinking about love makes us feel happy, doesn't it? Love means friends having fun. It means family celebrations. It means quiet time with Mom or Dad just before sleep. It means laughter, smiles, and warm feelings inside.

But . . . could it also possibly mean loving the meanest teacher you've ever had? Or lying down at night, closing your eyes, and praying for that kid who called you a freak? Surely not.

Surely—yes. That's exactly what Jesus means: "If you love those who love you, what credit is that to you? For even sinners love those who love them. If you do good to those who do good to you, what credit is that to you? For even sinners do the same" (Luke 6:32–33).

This is probably the hardest thing about this virtue we call charity. Loving the friends who love you back is nothing compared to loving the kid who seems dedicated to making your life miserable, and for no good reason.

Loving our enemies is probably the hardest thing about being friends with Jesus. Fortunately, we have lots of help. We have God's grace, ready for us if only we ask for it. We also have the saints—people who are ready to help us, and whose help means something special because so many of them found a way to love their enemies. Let's meet a few of them.

You know a lot about St. Patrick, of course. Did you know that as a young boy, St. Patrick was kidnapped from his home in England and taken to Ireland, where he was worked as a slave for six years? He escaped from slavery and traveled to France where he committed his life to serving God. When it was time for him to decide where he wanted to settle and work as a priest and a bishop, Patrick knew there was only one place to go, back to Ireland, the land of the very people who'd kept him as a slave. Why? Because he saw them with God's eyes, which are the eyes of love.

A few hundred years later, another Christian showed another kind of love for his enemies. Meinrad was a hermit monk who lived in what is now Switzerland. He was well known throughout the land as a holy man. But some thieves decided that the riches Meinrad had must be more than spiritual. These thieves came to visit Meinrad, who recognized them as notorious criminals. That didn't stop Meinrad, though, from welcoming the men with the love of Jesus in his heart, sharing his scarce food with them.

Such love, however, didn't stop the thieves—they went ahead and murdered St. Meinrad, and then found, of course, that his only riches were of the spirit.

Many Christians have been martyred by their own governments and societies throughout history. The early Christian martyrs who were killed by the Roman government always prayed for those who were imprisoning them and who would eventually kill them. Once again, a thousand years later, Christians were still being persecuted—in England this time. St. Edmund Campion was executed for being a Catholic in 1581. While he was in prison, he received and forgave the man who had betrayed him. On the day of his death, St. Edmund Campion stood on the platform where he was to be hung and, for his last words, told the crowd to pray that Queen Elizabeth, whose laws were responsible for his arrest and death, would have a long and happy reign!

St. Francis of Assisi lived during a time in which Christians and Muslims were often at war. These wars, called the Crusades, were battles for control of the sacred places in the Holy Land, and even, as time went on, the countries of Europe. St. Francis, of course, was a man of peace, and he wanted to do what he could to bring peace into these times of war. So St. Francis decided, for the first and only time in his life, to leave Italy and cross the sea to another country. He was going to visit an important Muslim leader and tell him about Jesus.

The leader was the sultan of a land called Babylonia. Although Christians and the Muslims of Babylonia were enemies, St. Francis didn't hesitate to travel in this dangerous land. He had no enemies—he loved all with the love of Jesus.

After a few unsuccessful attempts, St. Francis finally managed to visit the sultan, who received him with curiosity and even a little interest. He allowed Francis to visit him several times, and while he did not convert to Christianity, his own enemies criticized him from that point on for being too tolerant of Christians.

Sadly, many, many saints have been faced with the challenge of being despised by members of their own church. This tends to happen quite a bit to saints with new ideas. Leaders of all kinds, both in and out of the church, tend to be afraid of new ideas. They're afraid that the new ideas will get people too excited, and might even cause them to lose power—this fear of change is sad, but true.

St. Mary of the Cross MacKillop lived in Australia in the 1800s, when it was still a very wild place. She brought education to all parts of the untamed land and had a special love for the

Aborigines—who, much like Native Americans in this country, were the first residents of Australia. They were often treated very cruelly by Australian settlers. She was excommunicated—that is, forced to leave the church—for a whole year by her very own bishop after he had heard some false rumors about her!

St. John of the Cross was part of a movement in Spain in the sixteenth century to bring more discipline and seriousness to the lives of monks. Needless to say, many of the monks didn't like this very much, and St. John was kept imprisoned by them for months—twice!—as a way of discouraging him.

But what does it mean to love?

All of these people we're talking about managed to practice the virtue of charity, even toward those who hated and persecuted them. St. John shows us how. When he was dying, he was given a choice. He could spend his last days being cared for by a monk who was a friend of his or by a monk who had been his enemy for years.

He chose the monk who despised him. Not an easy choice, you can be sure. The choice didn't help the cruel monk see his wickedness at first, though. He continued to mistreat poor, dying John until one of his superiors heard what was going on and came to put a stop to it—the cruel monk then saw how wrong he had been and repented, his heart changed by the witness of John's love.

None of these saints would say it was easy to practice the virtue of charity, especially when they were called on to love an enemy. The price they paid was sometimes high. But if loving your enemies seems too much for you—and it's perfectly okay if it does seem that way—just think about what life would be like if these saints had just forgotten the virtue of charity and refused to love. Where is the power in that? Where is the good? How would the love of Jesus have spread if it hadn't been shared with the people who needed it most?

Venerable Pierre Toussaint

A Hero Lives a Life of Charity

Living in a world of grown-ups, a kid can be tempted to feel pretty small.

All the important things in life seem to belong to adults. They're the ones with the jobs and the cars. They're the ones who are in charge. The world runs on grown-up power, not kid power, it seems.

Not so fast. Remember, we're living in this world according to God's ways, and if you think about it, God's word isn't very

interested in the powers that run the world, except to sometimes tell them to shape up and do right.

Our friendship with God is the most important thing in our lives. And anyone can be friends with God, which means that anyone, no matter who or where they are, can see the world through God's eyes and love the world as he loves. Anyone can practice the virtue of charity.

No matter who you are or where you are in life, you can love God and love his people. Our saints let us see this clearly, because they come from all walks of life and from all over the world. One such saint is the Venerable Pierre Toussaint, who began his life as a slave.

Pierre was born around 1766 in Haiti, which is about one-third of an island in the Caribbean Sea. At this time, Haiti was one of the wealthiest places on earth. It was owned by the French, who grew rich from the sugar cane grown on the island. The whole world wanted sugar, as well as the drink called rum, which was made from sugar. Many people were willing to spend a lot of money on it.

Unfortunately, someone had to pay a price for this wealth. In Haiti, it was enslaved people from Africa who had been brought to work the land after disease killed off most of the island's indigenous peoples. Pierre was a descendent of these African slaves, but he was lucky because his owner, Monsieur Bérard, educated him, had him baptized, and treated him well.

In 1793, the slaves in Haiti were getting more and more dissatisfied, and it was clear that war would come soon. The Bérards moved to New York, and soon after they began what they had hoped would be a short stay, rebellion broke out back home. They heard the news that their plantation had been burned to the ground, and Monsieur Bérard died.

Madame Bérard was left without anything and anyone to help her. Except, of course, Pierre.

In New York, Pierre had been training in what you might think of as an unusual job: he'd been learning how to be a hairdresser. In those days, hairdressing was about a lot more than haircuts. If you can remember pictures you've seen of ladies during that time, you'll recall that hairstyles, especially for wealthy women, were very fancy, with hair stacked high, and lots of curls and ribbons hanging from the mountain of hair on their heads. It took skill to put a look like that together. It took time, and it took money. It seems as if Pierre was in just the right profession, after all.

From the time that Monsieur Bérard died, it was Pierre Toussaint who supported the family. He worked for sixteen hours a day, going from home to home, fixing the wealthy women's hair. The money he earned was enough to support the household until Madame Bérard died. When she died, she gave Pierre his freedom, and now, free of other obligations, Pierre was finally able to marry Juliette, the young woman he loved.

Of course, being a good hairdresser isn't what makes Pierre Toussaint a saint. During his long life, he was a strong witness to the love of God to all he met. He was completely dedicated to living the virtue of charity.

Pierre spoke of God's love and the beauty of the Catholic faith to his customers and others, most of whom weren't Catholic and many of whom didn't really like Catholics very much. He brought sick people into his home and cared for them. He went into neighborhoods devastated by fevers and plague, places where everyone else was too frightened to go, and brought help to the sick who had often been abandoned by their own families.

Mother Elizabeth Seton—another saint who lived in New York during this time—started an orphanage in 1817. Pierre Toussaint provided a great deal of the support for the orphanage. He gave of his own money and constantly collected donations from his customers.

Pierre and Juliette also were important in the founding of the first New York Catholic school for black children. And they supported a group of black women who were trying to form their own religious order of sisters.

When Pierre Toussaint died in 1853 at the age of eighty-seven, he was well-known in New York City for his love and generosity. The newspapers even carried articles about all he had done for the poor people of New York and how deep his love for God was. In a time when black people were treated badly, were bought and sold as property, and were seen as inferior to white people, it says a great deal about Pierre Toussaint's holiness and his importance in New York that the newspapers would even mention that he had died, much less offer him great praise!

Yes, the world is a big, busy place full of great need, and we are so small. All of us—grown-ups, too—wonder sometimes whether we can make a difference when we're just one person and the world is full of so many people who need God's love. The story of Venerable Pierre Toussaint teaches us to not wonder about such things and to not be discouraged by how the world sees us.

He was born a slave in the world's eyes, but through the virtue of charity that he shared with all he met, he brought the warmth of God's love into countless lives. No matter who we are or where we are, no matter how small the world tries to make us feel, we can always and everywhere practice the virtue of charity and share God's love with everyone in our life.

Rose Hawthorne Lathrop

A Hero Cares for Those Who Need It Most

When we're hurt, it's really nice if someone comes along to make it all better.

Sometimes a hurt can be fixed, and love helps you see that possibility and helps to make it happen. But other times, no matter how much love you have, no matter how vividly you're seeing the pain of someone else with the eyes of charity, or God's love, the problem that's causing the pain just can't be fixed.

When your best friend's parents are getting divorced and her heart is being ripped apart too, all the love you have for your friend isn't going to bring her household back together in the way she'd like. When your grandmother dies, there's nothing you can do to bring her back and bring instant happiness into your mom's tear-filled eyes.

There are some things—a lot of things, actually—that are way beyond our control. All the love, compassion, and charity in the world can't put things back together the way they were.

Still, Jesus calls us to love. But what does that mean when we can't fix the problem? Should we just give up and walk away?

Rose Hawthorne Lathrop wondered about that, too. Fortunately for hundreds of people, she came up with an answer that's still offering love and help today, many years after she died.

Rose's father is a very famous man—but don't worry if you haven't heard of him yet. You will soon enough—probably in your first English class in high school. His name was Nathaniel Hawthorne, and he was one of the greatest American writers. His two most well-known books are *The House of the Seven Gables* and *The Scarlet Letter.*

Rose, born in Massachusetts in 1851, was his youngest daughter. She led a very busy life as a girl, living all over Europe. When she was small, her family moved from America to live in England and Italy. (There's a story that when the family, which wasn't Catholic, by the way, was touring the Vatican gardens, little Rose got careless in her play and ran right into the pope!)

When Rose was thirteen, her father died, and her mother moved the family to Germany. A few years later, Rose met a young writer named George Lathrop. They fell in love, and although they were very young (Rose was twenty), they married in England and, three months later, moved back to the United States.

Rose's marriage quickly grew difficult. Her husband never really grew up, had a bad temper, and drank too much. They had a son, but he died when he was only four years old. This was all very hard on both the Lathrops, of course, and George's behavior just got worse and worse. In 1881, both Rose and George became Catholic, and for a time, their shared faith brought them closer together, but not for long. Eventually Rose began to fear for her safety, and to protect herself, she moved from Connecticut to New York City.

This was the start of a new life for Rose in many ways. She had endured some very hard times, but through it all, she was still filled with the love of Jesus. She had lost her husband and her child, but she still had God as her best friend, and she felt that he was calling her to use her life for good. But how?

The answer came through a friend, but it wasn't good news that Rose heard. Her very good friend Emma Lazarus (who wrote the poem on the tablet held by the Statue of Liberty) was dying. She was dying of cancer.

Emma's sickness made Rose think. You know that today there are some forms of cancer that are easy to treat, and others that are difficult or impossible to treat. In Rose Hawthorne's day, all cancer was incurable, and the deaths that people went through because of it were often quite horrible. Cancer is a disease in which cells grow uncontrollably and take over parts of the body. It is very painful, and if the cancer strikes the face (like the nose or the mouth), it can harm your facial features in ways that are not only painful but look frightening to others.

For this reason, as well as the fact that many people feared that cancer was contagious, cancer patients were often abandoned. Rose's friend Emma was wealthy and received good care, but Rose looked around her and saw that there were many others who were not so fortunate. In particular, the poor afflicted with cancer had nowhere to go. Once patients were diagnosed with incurable cancer, not even hospitals would take them. They preferred to take care of patients they could heal, not those that were going to die.

Understanding all of this, the call came loud and clear to Rose. She had found her mission of love and charity: to care for the poor afflicted with incurable cancer.

Rose's first step was to move to where the poor lived. She took a small apartment in one of the poorest sections of New York and used that as her home base. Every day, she would set out with bandages and ointments and whatever pain-killing medicines she could find, and she would visit the cancer patients in their homes.

Soon, Rose began taking the cancer patients into her apartment, and as you can imagine, she quickly ran out of room. Along with a friend, Rose began to raise money for larger quarters. They were eventually able to buy a house, and then, as time went on, with the help of many kind people (the writer Mark Twain gave Rose much support), she was able to buy another large home outside of New York City where her patients could go to live and die in the peace of the countryside.

By this time, Rose's husband, George, had died, so Rose and her friend Alice Huber decided to form a religious community especially dedicated to the care of these cancer patients. The religious order they formed still exists today—it's called the Dominican Sisters of Hawthorne, and they still run several homes for patients with incurable cancer. The care is totally free to the patients, and the sisters are all trained nurses who share the love of Jesus with those in pain.

So no, you can't fix everything. Rose Hawthorne probably wished she could have cured the cancer of every person she met. Love can make you feel that way. But love can also help you see what you can do when you can't fix the hurt. You can share the love of Jesus by simply being with others who are suffering and doing what you can to help them feel better.

Loving doesn't always mean fixing. Sometimes living the virtue of charity means just means doing what you can. And that's enough.

St. Teresa of Calcutta

A Hero Lives Charity with the Dying

If you had to pick out the most important thing you did this week, what would it be?

Making a B on a test you thought you'd failed? Protecting the goal on that last shot and saving the game? Convincing your mom to buy you that new outfit?

Was that it? Or might it be something else—a different kind of "important"?

Sometime, somehow in the last week, you've listened to someone who was sad or angry. You've defended someone who's been picked on. You bit your tongue when you wanted to mouth off to your dad. You thanked your mom for the dinner she fixed. You went through your clothes and picked out some good stuff to send to kids at the homeless shelter.

In other words, the most important thing you've done today, yesterday, and last week is love. One act of love, no matter how quiet, can change a person's day—even his or her whole life! Now that's important.

When we think about the difference that love can make, many people very often think of one person: St. Mother Teresa of Calcutta. A tiny woman, just under five feet tall, with no tools except prayer, love, and the unique qualities God had given her, Mother Teresa is probably the most powerful symbol of the virtue of charity for people today.

Mother Teresa wasn't, of course, born with that name. Her parents named her Agnes—or Gonxha in her own language—when she was born to them in Albania, a country north of Greece.

Agnes was one of four children. Her childhood was a busy, ordinary one. Although Agnes was very interested in missionary work around the world, as a child she didn't really think about becoming a nun; but when she turned eighteen, she felt that God was beginning to tug at her heart, to call her, asking her to follow him.

Now Agnes, like all of us, had a choice. She could have ignored the tug on her heart. She could have filled her life up with other things so maybe she wouldn't hear God's call. But of course, she didn't do that. She listened and followed, joining a religious order called the Sisters of Loreto, who were based in Dublin, Ireland.

After two months in Ireland, spent mostly learning how to speak English, Agnes got on a boat (in 1928, hardly anyone took trips by plane), and thirty-seven days later she arrived in the beautiful, busy, complicated country of India.

In India, Agnes took her final vows as a sister and took the name Teresa, after Thérèse of Lisieux, the Little Flower. She spent fifteen years teaching in a girl's school in Calcutta, a job that she loved and was very good at. But then one day, she heard that call again.

The voice in her heart was telling her that she was to make a very big change in her life—that she should leave her teaching position and go into the streets of Calcutta and care for the poor.

Again, Teresa could have ignored the voice and just gone on teaching the wealthy girls behind the high walls of her school. But you know how it feels to ignore the voice of God in your heart, right? You can't rest easy until you obey that voice. Do you know why?

It's not because God wants to play games with you or test you. No, it's because God created you and knows you better than anyone else does. He knows what all of your talents are and he knows what you can do with those talents. He also knows that he made you, above all, to love. That pull on your conscience is a nudge, giving you a hint about where you're going to find happiness and peace, and where the charity you practice is going to have the greatest impact.

So Sister Teresa listened and said yes. She had lived in India for years, and she knew how desperate the poor of that country were, especially in the big cities. It was these people, the dying poor, that Sister Teresa felt a special call to love. After all, these were people who had absolutely no one else in the world to love them. Not only were they poor, but they were also dying. Why did their feelings matter? Wouldn't they be gone soon enough?

Teresa saw these people differently. She saw them through God's eyes, which means that she saw each of them as his dear child, suffering and yearning for some kind touch or word, some comfort in their last days on earth. She heard that call and chose to live it out—to let God love the forgotten ones through her charity.

As is the case with all great things, Teresa's efforts started out small. She got permission to leave her order, to live with the poor, and to dress like them, too. She changed her habit from the traditional one to the sari worn by Indian women. Her sari would be white with blue trim, the blue symbolizing the love of Mary. She didn't waste time, either. On her very first day among the poor of Calcutta, Mother Teresa started a school with five students, a school for poor children. That school still exists today. She quickly got some training in basic medical care and went right into the homes of the poor to help them.

Within two years, Teresa had been joined by other women in her efforts, all of them her former students. She was soon "Mother Teresa" because she was the head of a new religious order: the Missionaries of Charity.

The Missionaries of Charity tried to care for as many of the dying as they could. They bought an old Hindu temple and made it into what they called a home for the dying. Hospitals had no room or interest in caring for the dying—especially the dying poor—so the dying had no choice but to lie on the streets and suffer. The sisters knew this, so they didn't wait for the poor to come to them. They constantly roamed the streets, picking up what looked from the outside like nothing but a pile of rags, but was actually a sick child or a frail old person.

When a dying person came or was brought to Mother Teresa and her sisters, they were met with nothing but love. They were washed and given clean clothes, medicine, and—most important—someone who could hold their hand, listen, stroke their foreheads, and comfort them with love in their last days.

One of the most feared diseases in the world is leprosy. It's a terrible sickness that deadens a person's nerves and can even cause their fingers, toes, ears, and nose to eventually fall away. You know that in Jesus' time, lepers were kept away from communities. Lepers in poor countries like India, where they have a hard time getting the medicines to treat the disease, are often treated the same way.

You can probably guess what Mother Teresa thought and—more important—what she did about this. After all, a person with leprosy isn't a thing or an animal with no feelings. A person with leprosy is, above all, a person whom God loves and cares deeply about.

So Mother Teresa saw people with leprosy in the same way—through God's loving eyes. She got the help of doctors and nurses, gathered lepers from the slums, and began treating and caring for them in a way that no one before her had tried to do.

Mother Teresa's work of love started out small, but it isn't small anymore. There are more than four thousand Missionaries of Charity today, living, praying, and caring for the helpless in more than a hundred different houses around the world, including in the United States.

Mother Teresa died in 1997, but even now, when we think about her work, we can learn all we need to know about love: It doesn't take any money or power to love. It doesn't take great talent or intelligence. It simply takes love.

St. Teresa of Calcutta did wonderful, brave work in caring for the forgotten, but if there's one thing she would want you to remember about love, it's that you don't have to travel to foreign countries to practice the virtue of charity. In fact, love has to start where you live:

> It is easy to love those who live far away. It is not always easy to love those who live right next to us. It is easier to offer a dish of rice to meet the hunger of a needy person than to comfort the loneliness and the anguish of someone in our own home who does not feel loved. I want you to go and find the poor in your homes. Above all, your love has to start there. (Mother Teresa, *No Greater Love,* [Novato, Calif.: New World Library, 1997], p. 27.)

Temperance

The fruit of the Spirit
is love, . . . gentleness, and self-control.

Galatians 5:22–23

Jesus Strikes a Balance

Is the world and all the stuff in it good or bad?

Have you been put here on earth to get the most fun you can out of life? Or were you born to just resist the temptation of all that fun stuff until the day God lets you escape?

Throughout history, and even today, people have different opinions about the world and our place in it. Some people believe, and then try to convince you through commercials, television shows, and even music, that the best way to live your life is to just have a lot of fun and get all the enjoyment out of the world that you can.

Others think it would be better if you would just stay completely away from all of those same commercials, shows, and music, not to mention other people who might be considered "bad."

What's a Christian kid to do? There's an answer—there always is, you know—and the answer is in the same place it always is: in Jesus. When you look at the life of Jesus, you see miracles and you hear parables. But you also see something else: you see Jesus enjoying life at the very same time that he's telling us to be ready to give it up, if necessary.

What you see is Jesus showing us what the virtue called temperance is all about. *Temperance* is a big word, but it has a pretty simple meaning. Remember it this way: A temperate climate is one in which the weather isn't too hot or too cold. It's just right, just in the middle, all the time.

So, using our great brains, we can figure out that when we live out the virtue of temperance, we're in the middle, too. We're not tricked into thinking that stuff like food, drink, entertainment, and other kinds of fun can make us happy all by themselves, and we know that too much of any of that can hurt us. But on the other hand, we're not afraid of those things, either.

In other words, when we practice the virtue of temperance, we put everything in its place. We're not afraid of the things that God has made or helped us to make, but we don't mistake those things for God in our lives, either.

Let's look at Jesus to see how this works.

Some people might tell you that enjoying things like food and drink is bad. But Jesus shows us that it's not. A lot of Gospel stories show us Jesus enjoying meals—parties, really. He was criticized by some religious leaders of his day for this very thing. They thought it was wrong that he and his disciples didn't fast—that is, eat very little—like they thought holy people should do. They were surprised—and not in a good way—that Jesus went to meals and parties at the homes of well-known sinners like Zaccheus.

Jesus uses meals in his stories, too. When he wanted to explain what the kingdom of God was like, he used a banquet as his example. In the parable of the prodigal son, the first thing the father does when he sees his sorry son heading back home is to order up a party.

And don't forget what John tells us Jesus' first miracle was: He changed water into wine at a wedding feast!

So it seems pretty clear that for Jesus enjoying friends and food is a really good thing. Being a friend of Jesus doesn't mean cutting yourself off from the world. It means plunging right into it, just like he did. It means bringing God's love into every one of those situations, just like he did.

But on the other hand . . . (You knew there would be another hand, right?)

Jesus also warns us not to get the wrong idea about the wonderful things in God's world. He tells us not to worry about the stuff we have, or to spend too much time getting more stuff. He tells us that God will take care of us: God takes care of the lilies of the field, right (Luke 12:22–34)?

Jesus tells parables about foolish people who go too far in their enjoyment of life. There's the parable of the rich fool who spends his whole life building up great treasures for himself on earth and storing them in a barn. The problem is that this fellow has forgotten that he will die someday—"this very night," God tells him—

and that he won't be able to take one single thing in that barn with him.

Jesus also tells us that, if necessary, we must be ready at any moment to sacrifice all of the pleasures and safety of the world for the sake of truth and love. And that does happen, you know. We're called to make choices like that all the time: Should I spend my money on myself or on helping a poor person? Should I dedicate my life to having fun or could I use my talents to help some suffering people?

It's a balancing act. The world God created is good. The things that human beings create from God's raw materials can be used for good or bad. Jesus calls us to practice the virtue of temperance—to use all of what God has given us to help us grow toward him. We should never forget that since God is our best friend, it's really a sham, or worse, to go crazy with the fun of the moment and forget who gave this great life to us in the first place—and why.

Peter and Cornelius

Heroes Love Their Neighbors, No Matter What

"You are what you eat."

Really? Let's hope not. You don't really want to be that cherry cola and bag of corn chips you had for breakfast, do you?

Most of us love food, but you might have noticed that figuring out the right way to think about food can be hard. Should you see food as your best friend, eating whatever you want whenever you want it? Well, no, not unless you want to get out of shape and sick.

Should you see food as your enemy because it has the power to make you weigh more than the bony models in the magazines? No again—unless, of course you want to get sick and be focused on the wrong things.

Food is everywhere. It tastes good and can change the way we look and feel, for better or for worse. That's why the temptation to build our world around food is strong. Sometimes we're tempted to see food as our comfort and eat whenever we're sad or angry or even bored. But sometimes we might think that if we don't eat anything (or if we eat just a tiny little bit), then we'll be a better person.

You can see that when it comes to food, temperance is pretty important. Going to either extreme—too much or too little—harms us. Going to either extreme tempts us to think more about food and its effects on our body than we think about God's place in our lives. We look to food for comfort when we're sad instead of looking to God. We avoid a normal healthy diet because we forget that it's our friendship with God, not our weight, that makes us a better person.

Not long after the church began, the early Christians struggled with the question of food, believe it or not. Now, in many ways their struggles were different from what you're facing; they weren't worried about how food made them look. But that said, the basic questions beneath the early Christians' and our own difficulties are the same: As Christians, what role should food play in our life? Does our attitude toward food affect our relationship with God?

As you probably remember, most of the earliest Christians were also Jewish. They had been raised in the Jewish faith, and were filled with joy because Jesus was the Messiah their people had been awaiting for centuries. They also lived by the Jewish Law.

The Law is what we call the guidelines for life that God gave the Jewish people during the time of Moses. The Law deals with almost every part of life, from how to treat your children, to how to deal with criminals, to what to eat.

The Law begins with the Ten Commandments. It also includes many other laws, which you can find in the books of Exodus, Leviticus, and Deuteronomy in the Old Testament. The

Law has very specific rules on what a faithful Jewish person could eat. They could not, for example, eat pork or shellfish, and the other meats they could eat had to be slaughtered in a certain way.

All of this had a very good purpose. It was a way for God to help the Jewish people understand how special they were. It helped them show the world through every action that they belonged to the one, true God and no one else.

For a few years after Pentecost, these rules worked out fine for the new Christian community because it was made up of people who were also Jewish. But then people who weren't Jewish started becoming Christians. As Christians, should they have to obey Jewish laws?

The apostle Peter was one of the first to confront this problem when he met with a man named Cornelius. Cornelius lived on the coast of what is now Israel. He was a Roman. He admired the Jewish people, but he was not one of them. He was a pagan. One day, an angel came to Cornelius and told him to invite a man named Peter to his home—so he did.

At the very same time, in another place, Peter was having the strangest dream. He dreamed that a big white sheet was being lowered from heaven. On that sheet were all of the animals of the world—those that he, as a Law-abiding Jewish-Christian man, was permitted to eat, but also those animals that were forbidden. Acts 10:13–16 describes part of Peter's dream.

> Then he heard a voice saying, "Get up, Peter; kill and eat." But Peter said, "By no means, Lord; for I have never eaten anything that is profane or unclean." The voice said to him again, a second time, "What God has made clean, you must not call profane." This happened three times, and the thing was suddenly taken up to heaven.

So of course, Peter had this on his mind when he went to Cornelius's house. It must have been a strange moment, don't you think? Each man had had this strange experience, but neither knew what it could possibly have to do with the other guy. But when Peter met Cornelius and heard that his invitation to visit had come directly from God, Peter made the connection.

Peter, as a Jew, really shouldn't have even been in Cornelius's house at all. It was one of those things that the Law prohibited. And if Peter shouldn't have even been in the house, you can imagine how "illegal" it would have been for him to share a meal with Cornelius and his family.

So Peter told the whole household of his dream, and then told them about Jesus. He said that he understood that the reason he'd been given that dream was so that he would know that Jesus had come for everyone, not just for the Jewish people. He realized that there shouldn't be any barriers between anyone who accepts Jesus, especially barriers over food.

Right there, Cornelius and his whole family were baptized.

The news of Peter's meal made many Jewish Christians very angry. The arguments over the Law got so bad that an important meeting had to be called in Jerusalem—at that time, still the center of Christianity—to try to sort everything out. If this meeting, called the Council of Jerusalem, had failed to find an answer to this crisis, the growth of Christianity could have been stopped in its tracks, right then and there.

But, led by Peter and Paul, the apostles and others decided that Gentiles (non-Jews) who wanted to become Christian wouldn't have to obey what the Jewish Law said about food, except that they shouldn't eat meat from animals that had been sacrificed to pagan gods or that had been improperly slaughtered. This decision allowed Christianity to keep growing.

Now, what does all of this have to do with you and your after-school snack?

The early Christians had to think long and hard about the proper role of food in their lives. They finally decided that they didn't want to let food stand in people's way to God.

Your decisions aren't exactly the same, but you can still take this first lesson in the virtue of temperance and make it work for you. Food can stand in our way to God, too. We can misuse food and hurt the bodies God gave us in a lot of ways. Temperance teaches us to put God first—and use the food he's blessed us with as one way to help make us stronger for him!

Charlemagne and Alcuin

Heroes Use Their Talents for Good

Nice brain you've got there. You can do a lot with it: write stories, design bridges, cure diseases, compose music, plan robberies, weave lies to stay out of trouble. . . . Wait a minute. What's with those last two items on the list?

Well, everything on that list is about thinking. It's about all the things that can come out of your brain. And like it or not, we can use our brains for bad just as easily as we can for good. You can use that mind, your hand, and a piece of paper to write a note

of welcome to a new kid in the class or a note to your friends wondering why the new kid is so weird.

Same brain. Same hand. Same paper. Much different results, right?

The mind and imagination that God gave you are amazing gifts. They can go in any direction you choose. It might be good to practice the virtue of temperance when you're making your decision which way to go. Remember that temperance is the virtue of using what God has given us in the proper, balanced way, and making sure that our use of the things of this world is always directed toward the good.

Face it—you can use that brain you have to hatch a million mean, dishonest, and just plain sneaky plots. But just because you can, should you? You could be focusing your brain power on how to make life easiest and most fun for you and you alone, no matter how it hurts other people. But just because you can, should you?

Hundreds of years ago, Europe was a mess. Yes, we're back to the Dark Ages again, but near the end of it this time. Much-needed light is about to shine in the darkness of war, poverty, and ignorance. Someone is about to use their brain power to do some good.

Throughout the 600s and 700s, one particular tribe of people gained a great deal of power and land throughout Western Europe. That tribe was called the Franks, and if you think for a minute (there's that brain power again!), you just might be able to figure out where the name of the country France came from. Got it? Good for you!

One of the great leaders of the Franks was Charles Martel. His son had a funny name—Pepin the Short. However strange Pepin the Short's name is, you've probably heard of his son—Charles the Great, or as we call him today, Charlemagne.

Charlemagne ruled the Frankish people, expanded their kingdom throughout Western Europe, and was even given the title of Emperor of the West by the pope in the year 800. Charlemagne was in charge of a lot of land and a lot of people. What would he do with all of this?

You've heard about kings who have used their power selfishly. Charlemagne lived in a violent, brutal time, so he had his violent, brutal moments like almost everyone else. But what set Charlemagne apart from other rulers, and why we remember him today, is that Charlemagne was very, very committed to learning.

You see, Charlemagne wanted his empire to honor God. He also felt very strongly that people could best honor and love God when they understood him. So Charlemagne decided to make education the first job of his kingdom. But since he himself, sad to say, could barely read or write, he had to put someone else in charge of the job. The man he put in charge was named Alcuin.

Blessed Alcuin had been born in England and was in charge of a school there. He met Charlemagne while he was returning from Rome to England, and the king asked him to start a school for him. Alcuin was impressed by Charlemagne's seriousness, so he agreed.

Alcuin's school was located in Charlemagne's palace in a town called Aachen. Everyone who lived in the palace was encouraged to come to the school to learn to read, write, and think clearly and logically. Even the emperor, Charlemagne, came to the school!

Alcuin was also put in charge of the kingdom's books. You remember, of course, that Charlemagne and Alcuin lived hundreds of years before the printing press was invented, so every single book that was made had to be copied by hand. Alcuin wrote a guidebook for copyists to help them make sure they did their work right. He also came up with a new way of writing that was faster because with it, you could link the letters together. You know the system as cursive, and yes, Alcuin invented it. Now you know who to blame!

It's said, by the way, that Charlemagne got into the habit of always having a tablet or some parchment (dried animal skin that was used like paper) under his pillow so that when he was resting, if he felt like it, he could practice writing. It didn't do much good, though—the person who wrote Charlemagne's life story admitted that the king started learning too late and never really got very good at his letters.

Alcuin threw himself into planning out the palace school, and when that was established, he dedicated himself to helping Charlemagne's other dream come true: a system of schools throughout the kingdom, with one attached to every monastery and cathedral.

(It's strange to imagine a country without schools, isn't it? But that's the way it was back then. It sounds fun, but you might want to think twice before trying any time travel. You might not be in school, but you would be in the fields from sunup to sundown, or in the shop doing carpentry, weaving, or blacksmithing. Does school really sound so bad now?)

Alcuin was totally dedicated to education because he agreed with Charlemagne that learning to think and understand was an excellent way to honor God. It was through reading and writing, Alcuin believed, that we could spread the faith and understand the faith, and then, through art and music, we could celebrate our friendship with God. Both Charlemagne and Alcuin believed that when a country was filled with people using their minds this way—for the good—that country would be peaceful and happy.

So there it is—one brain given to you to use during one lifetime. You can do good with it—or you can do bad. The virtue of temperance helps you figure out how to do it: treating life with balance and always using the gifts God has given you for good, and not for evil and selfishness.

Which is it going to be?

St. Francis

A Hero Appreciates Creation

Life is full of fun stuff to do. There are school and hobbies to keep you busy. There's television to watch, computer and video games to play, music to listen to, movies to go to. There are amusement parks, ball games, and museums to enjoy.

But even with all of this human-made stuff to fill our lives, you have to admit there's nothing like the ocean, or a billion stars splashed over a quiet night sky, or even just the silence and perfection of newly fallen snow.

There's something special about nature, isn't there? It's a beautiful gift from God that we've been given that enables us to live. It's also been given to us to enjoy, appreciate, and protect.

Taking care of the earth is not a new idea. It's as old as God's gift of the earth to Adam and Eve. Ever since, holy people have understood that the earth isn't to be used, torn up, and destroyed. They've understood that it's a gift from God, and we owe it to God to take care of this gift. They've understood that when it comes to the earth, it's good to live according to the virtue of temperance.

Temperance teaches us that, when it comes to the earth, the middle is just where we need to be. We shouldn't destroy God's creation, but we shouldn't be afraid to use it appropriately when we need to, either.

There's one saint who, more than any other, teaches us about the precious gift of creation. Even people who aren't Christians treasure the lessons this man taught. He's so strongly connected with nature that people even put statues of him in their gardens!

We're talking, of course, about St. Francis of Assisi. St. Francis is famous for many things. He's famous for leaving a life of wealth to embrace poverty. He's well known for deciding to live as Jesus did and to serve the poor as one of them. He's known for making the Christmas nativity scene popular, and he's remembered for the gift of the stigmata—the wounds of Jesus—that he received on his body.

But St. Francis is also famous for his love of nature and for the love that creation, in turn, had for him. Why did St. Francis love nature so much? Because it's beautiful? Because it helps us live? No, that's not why. St. Francis loved creation because God had made it. Every single flower was the work of God's hands and God's love—so of course St. Francis had to care for it!

St. Francis would move worms off the road so they wouldn't be run over or walked on. He fed bees honey and wine in the winter months, when the flowers were not in bloom. A cicada—a kind of insect that makes a loud humming noise—lived outside of St. Francis's little home. St. Francis often held the cicada on his finger and asked it to sing for him.

Once, a man sent a pheasant—a kind of bird—to St. Francis. We can assume that he expected the bird to be cooked and eaten by the beggar brothers. That's not what St. Francis had in mind at all. He welcomed the bird as "Brother Pheasant" and told the brothers to take the bird out to the forest to see whether it wanted to be free or return to live with them.

Of course, the bird returned right to St. Francis and his brothers again and again, and from that moment he was St. Francis's special friend.

One of the best-known stories about St. Francis involves a creature much more frightening than a worm or a bird. It's about the wolf of Gubbio.

Gubbio was a village that was being terrorized by a large, terrible wolf. This wolf didn't just eat other animals. It attacked people. It was so vicious that none of the villagers would go near the woods where the wolf lived without carrying weapons for protection.

St. Francis felt bad for the people of Gubbio and wanted to help them. He set out to meet the wolf. The people of the village went a short distance with him, but they became too frightened to go any farther. St. Francis told them that it was all right, he would go alone. The villagers told him to take weapons, but he told them that all he needed was God's protection.

The wolf came in sight. It raced toward Francis, its mouth open. Francis stood without fear and made the sign of the cross in the direction of the wolf. It stopped in its tracks, and St. Francis said, "Come unto me, Brother Wolf. In the name of Christ, I order you not to hurt me or anyone."

So the wolf came, lowered its head, and lay down at St. Francis's feet. Francis kept on talking to the wolf. He told the wolf that it had done terrible things and that it really did deserve to have its life taken for the hurt it had brought to the village. But Francis was going to give the wolf one more chance. If it promised not to hurt anyone else—human or animal—the villagers would not harm the wolf and would, in fact, see to it that it would be fed.

The wolf, the story goes, moved its body, tail, and ears to show that it agreed, and then put its paw gently into Francis's open hand. St. Francis said, "Brother Wolf, I order you, in the name of the Lord Jesus Christ, to come with me now, without fear, into the town to make this peace pact in the name of the Lord."

Of course, the villagers were amazed and frightened, but when St. Francis explained to them what had happened, they agreed that for the rest of the wolf's days, they would care for it. The wolf lived for two years after that, and during that time, it didn't hurt anyone, the villagers fed it, and even the dogs left it alone.

When we think about the virtues that our saints and holy friends of God live by, we might think that they're only concerned with how to treat other human beings. The stories of St. Francis and the natural world show that when we love God, we love all that he's made—the people, the animals, and even the trees, the oceans, and the mountains. The virtue of temperance teaches us how. It teaches us how to treat nature in a balanced way: to use it properly, the way God intended, and to honor nature, not for itself, but because it comes from God's hand. Then we can pray along with St. Francis the prayer that he wrote:

> Praised be you, Lord, with all that you have made,
> And first my Lord Brother sun,
> Who brings the day;
>
> All praise be yours, my Lord, through Sister Moon
> and stars
> In the heavens you have made them, bright and
> precious and fair.
>
> All praise be yours, my Lord, through Sister Earth, our
> mother.
> Who feeds us in her sovereignty and produces
> Various fruits with colored flowers and herbs.
>
> Praise and bless my Lord, and give him thanks
> And serve him with great humility!
>
> (*Catholic Source Book* [Worthington, Minn.: The Printers, 1980], 25.)

VENERABLE MATT TALBOT

Heroes Can Let Go

Where did the time go, anyway? It was only a few minutes ago—right after breakfast, in fact—that you sat down in front of that computer game. So, why is it dark outside? Why is your mom banging on the door asking if you're all right. And why are your fingers stuck in that weird curled-up position?

Sounds to me like you've got a bit of an addiction.

You probably know what the word *addiction* means, but let's make sure. An addiction is a dependence on something outside yourself. When you're addicted to something, you come to believe

that you need that thing to be happy and at peace. In other words, you feel as though you can't live without it.

All addictions end up in the same place: your body, including your brain, which needs that outside thing to feel okay. Addictions don't all start in the same place, though. Some are rooted somehow in the way that our bodies react chemically to certain things. But some addictions start in our own choices. We can get addicted to all kinds of things: playing computer and video games, surfing the Internet, being with another person, gossiping, eating. We can get addicted to the feeling of winning or of always being the best student.

Wherever the addictions come from, they all lead to the very same result: putting something else in God's place. That's why temperance is such an important virtue. It helps us put everything in the right place in our lives: to enjoy what God has given us, but not to live for the enjoyment of those things.

The most serious addictions of all are, of course, addictions to alcohol and drugs. People who are addicted to these things bear a terrible burden of sadness and frustration. Many would like to be free, but releasing themselves from the prison of alcohol or drugs is very, very hard and very, very scary.

Fortunately, we have Matt Talbot to show us that it can be done.

Matt Talbot was born into a poor Irish family in 1856. In those days, young people had to go to work very early in life to help support their families. In Matt's case, sad to say, the only job he could find was working on a boat dock, unloading cases of wine.

You won't be surprised to learn that in the course of a day, wine bottles were broken and cracked. You might also not be surprised to learn that the workers would often take advantage of this situation and sneak a drink when this happened. All of Matt's coworkers did this, so Matt started doing the same thing. He was twelve years old.

By the time Matt was thirteen, he was seriously addicted to alcohol. His family eventually noticed, and Matt's father made him change jobs. Matt responded by changing drinks: from wine to whiskey. For the next sixteen years, when he wasn't working,

Matt was drinking. He drank heavily at pubs every night. Matt's health started to get worse, and he started finding it difficult to get up in the morning and go to work.

Don't get the idea that this was all one big party. It wasn't. Matt was very unhappy. He saw life through a fog and wanted desperately to clear that fog, but he was afraid of what would happen. Chronic, or serious, alcoholics begin to need the alcohol in order for their bodies to work, and if they stop drinking, they get very sick, with bad headaches and shakes for a long time until their bodies get back to normal.

Matt wanted to stop drinking, but he was afraid of what would happen to his body, and he was afraid of facing life as it was without drinking. He couldn't imagine real life without alcohol.

So one day, Matt made a very, very hard choice. He decided to stop. He knew it would be difficult and painful, but he also knew that if he didn't make that choice, life would only get worse and worse.

Since the choice would be so hard, Matt knew that he couldn't walk down that road all by himself. So he found a priest who listened to him and who encouraged him. He told the priest what he wanted and hoped for, and the priest said he would help Matt. He told Matt to start small by promising not to drink alcohol for three months.

The three months looked like an eternity, but Matt wanted to be happy. He wanted to be himself, not what the drinking made him. He wanted to be close to God. So he made the promise to himself, the priest, and most important, to God.

Matt started going to Mass every morning before work. He prayed other kinds of prayers like rosaries and novenas. He took a different path to and from work every day, avoiding the pubs and his drinking companions. He filled up his time with reading, especially books about the lives of the saints. When he felt weak, he went to the church and prayed in the presence of Jesus in the Eucharist. Matt let God into his life, and God, who is stronger than our worst addiction, helped Matt.

Matt was twenty-eight when he made the promise. With God's help he kept it until he died in 1925, at the age of sixty-eight. Matt was still very poor when he died, and he only had a few friends. But somehow, over time, his story began to spread. Today many shelters, homes, and other groups are named after him. The people who work in these places and with these groups help alcoholics and drug addicts, as well as homeless and poor people. In 1973, the church gave Matt Talbot the title of Venerable as a recognition of his holiness and as the first step to maybe being declared a saint!

That's a long road—from a boy whose life was almost ruined by addiction to a man who shines with hope for anyone who finds themselves in that prison.

Many things can make us happy for a moment, and that's perfectly okay. God gave us those things, and he wants us to have fun and enjoy them. But when we step over that thin line and start depending on those things to bring us happiness and get us through the day (like when you say, "I'll be happy when I get home from school and can shut my door to my family and just be on the computer all night!"), we're cutting ourselves off from the deeper, more satisfying happiness God has to give.

It's hard to stop, sure. But when we practice the virtue of temperance and balance our lives in little ways—and follow the lead of Venerable Matt Talbot—God will always help us. God is stronger than any of that stuff. He really is—but we don't know that until we ask him!

Blessed Pier Giorgio Frassati

A Hero Enjoys the Gift of Life

Is it really okay to have fun? Is it okay to stay up late with your friends, playing games, or singing along to the radio, and getting really, really silly? Is it okay to spend the afternoon playing football or basketball, running hard, laughing hard, and wearing yourself out? Is it okay to go to the movies, enjoy music, and have a blast at a pool party?

It's probably natural to just burst out "Of course!" to all of those questions, but there might be a little, tiny part of you that

still wonders. Sometimes kids get the idea that the words *fun* and *Christian* don't go together.

Sometimes kids worry that being friends with God means being really serious all the time. They think that if God's first, that means there isn't room for anything else, like fun.

Well, that's just not true, and it all comes down to that virtue called temperance. It means that you have to find balance and learn the difference between playing video games for an hour with some friends and playing video games locked up alone in your room for eight hours.

Temperance means knowing when to stop, knowing what attitude to have, and most of all, knowing when to put everything aside and spend quiet time with God.

Think this is impossible? Not at all. For proof, look at the short, but full, life of Blessed Pier Giorgio Frassati.

Pier Frassati was born in Italy in 1901. His father was involved in politics, and his mother was an artist. Pier didn't want for anything growing up. He had it all—comfort and more, the opportunity to travel and enjoy every kind of entertainment, and a family that cared for him.

Even though his parents weren't very interested in religion, they gave Pier and his sister an education in the Catholic faith anyway. Pier responded very strongly to the message of Jesus from a very early age.

Since Jesus had given Pier everything—life on earth and life with Jesus forever in heaven—Pier wanted to do something in return. Not because he was afraid of Jesus or because someone else made him, but because he loved Jesus and *wanted* to.

Remember that *faith* is really another word for having a friendship with God. If you have a friend whom you love and admire, you might try to imitate the more admirable parts of that friend—the way he can stay calm no matter what happens, the way she can balance her busy life. Well, it's the same with Jesus—when we look at Jesus, we see a lot to admire and love. There's really no one more worthy imitating, is there?

That's the way Pier felt. So as he grew older, he devoted a lot of time to deepening his friendship with Jesus by going to Mass every day, saying the rosary at least once a day, and even going to church at night to pray with Jesus in the Eucharist.

And when Pier looked at this Jesus whom he was coming to love more and more, he saw many things that he wanted to try to bring into his own life. What struck him most strongly was Jesus' love for the poor.

Pier was born into a wealthy family, and his friendship with Jesus taught him that this brought a great deal of responsibility with it. Pier wondered why he should have so much when others had nothing. Did he really need all the money and treats that he was given?

So Pier started giving. And giving and giving.

When he was a young boy, a poor mother and her barefoot son came begging at Pier's family home. Pier gave the boy his shoes, on the spot. Pier received an allowance from his father, which, most of the time, he turned around and gave to a poor person. If he was given money to ride the trolley (an old-fashioned kind of bus or train), very often he would give the coins away to a beggar, and then have to run all the way home from wherever he was because his father was very strict about his being on time for dinner!

Pier attended college, and instead of following in his father's footsteps of politics or newspaper writing, Pier studied the science and engineering of mines so that he could spend his career working with miners. Miners have one of the most dangerous, dirtiest jobs anyone could have—digging for minerals underneath the ground. When Pier graduated, his father gave him a choice of a gift: a car or money. You can probably guess what Pier chose, and what he did with the gift. You're right. He chose the money, and as quickly as he received it, he gave it away.

Pier also understood that helping the poor by giving them money is a good start, but it isn't enough. Many people were poor because their companies didn't pay them the wages they deserved or because other rules of government kept them poor. Pier was a part of groups dedicated to changing those rules. He often was a part of protests in the streets, protests that were often broken up by the police in very violent ways. Pier held his own. He wasn't afraid to defend himself and his right to speak for the truth, and he spent a few nights in jail as a result.

You may think that all of this is very admirable but sounds pretty grim. You're wrong. Pier Frassati had a very enjoyable life. First of all, remember that there's a great deal of joy to be found in helping the poor.

Second, Pier Frassati was a handsome, athletic, fun-loving guy. He had loads of friends and was always doing fun things with them—and to them, as well. He was a great practical joker. He loved the theater and music concerts. Most of all, he loved the outdoors. Turin, the town in Italy where he was born and lived, is in the northern part of Italy, close to the Alps. So of course, one of Pier's favorite pastimes was skiing.

He had a group of friends that he called "The Sinister Ones." They even had a silly motto to describe themselves, which is best translated into English as "The few, the proud . . . the macaroni!" Pier would lead his friends on energetic, dangerous mountain-climbing trips, followed by skiing trips back down the mountains that were just as energetic and just as dangerous.

Pier spent a great deal of time visiting the sick, and in 1925, he visited someone suffering from a disease called polio. Pier caught the disease himself, and it soon became very clear that it was a serious case. Knowing that he might die, Pier showed his family the account book he kept of all the families he helped—including the support of a widow and her three children—and begged them to make sure these people weren't forgotten.

Five days after he caught polio, Pier Frassati died at only twenty-four years of age. A few years later, people began to ask church leaders to look into Pier's life of holiness and care. The people who asked, by the way, were the poor people of Turin, and they were quite sure that Pier was a saint. In 1990, the church agreed, giving Pier the title of Blessed, which is just one step away from being called a Saint.

It was a short life, but what a full one! Pier's life was full of love and compassion, strong beliefs, work, and a lot of fun, too. If we want to understand what the virtue of temperance is, the story of Pier Frassati's life is a great place to look. Pier knew that there was nothing wrong with having fun and enjoying the world God has created—as long as you never forget who's first, at work or at play.

Prudence

Wisdom is better than might.

Ecclesiastes 9:16

Jesus Gives Us Leaders to Help Us Make Good Choices

Making the right decision can be really hard sometimes.

A friend of yours has been in a really bad mood lately. Everyone's talking about how mean she's been, and some people are starting to leave her out of activities because of how she acts.

The trouble is that this friend has shared a secret with you: Her parents are getting divorced, and it's making her miserable. But she's sworn you to secrecy—she doesn't want anyone to know.

Should you keep the secret? Or should you let everyone know what's going on so they can understand her mood? What do you do? And how do you decide what's best?

Prudence, that's how. When we practice the virtue called prudence, we make wise decisions, not based on what we feel like doing or what we're afraid will happen to us, but based on what God knows is best for us to do, right here and right now.

Prudent girls or boys make careful decisions about life, always considering God's love above everything else. They do this, not because they're afraid or because they've been told to, but because they trust God. God made us, God loves us, and God wants us to be happy. So it makes sense that living by his word will bring us happiness, and moving away from him will just make us miserable.

So how do you practice this virtue? How do know what God wants? Well, you can pray. You can listen to your conscience—not your emotions or desires, but your conscience: what your heart tells you is right.

Other people can help us figure out what's right, too. If we're serious about practicing the virtue of prudence, we just have to get used to listening to wise people: friends who've been through the same experience, parents, teachers, and our religious leaders.

In other words, in making these difficult decisions, it's a really good idea to turn to leaders and guides for help.

Jesus knew this, of course. As he walked the roads and the countryside of Palestine, sharing the good news of God's love with everyone he met, Jesus knew that his time on earth would eventually end. He knew that if the Good News was to continue being preached, he needed people to preach it. He needed people who would listen to him, learn from him, and then share his word with others for years to come. He needed leaders.

Jesus didn't go to the government to find these leaders. He didn't even go to schools to dig them up. He walked by the shore of a lake.

> As he walked by the Sea of Galilee, he saw two brothers, Simon, who is called Peter, and Andrew his brother, casting a net into the sea—for they were fishermen. And he said to them, "Follow me, and I will make you fish for people." Immediately they left their nets and followed him. As he went from there, he saw two other brothers, James son of Zebedee and his brother John, in the boat with their father Zebedee, mending their nets, and he called them. Immediately they left the boat and their father, and followed him. (Matthew 4:18–22)

Fishermen. Those were the first leaders he selected. Later, Jesus invited more to follow him, none of them important or famous, and at least one, Matthew (or Levi), who was in a particularly hated profession: tax collector!

Now, these leaders—called Jesus' apostles—weren't perfect. Not even close. They had dumb arguments among themselves about who was the most important. They tried to keep little children away from Jesus. They spent months and months with Jesus, and still, by the end of his life, didn't seem to really get what he was saying.

But despite the way it seems, Jesus obviously knew what he was doing, for after his ascension into heaven, the apostles received the Holy Spirit at Pentecost, and everything came together for them. What had been unclear became clear. What had seemed weak became strong. Just as Jesus said it would be, the Good News was spread to the entire world. Jesus' church had the leaders it needed, the leaders who would pass on Jesus' teaching and help the people of the world understand it and make good decisions based on its truth.

Some time after Pentecost, a man named Philip, who had joined the apostles in Jerusalem, was walking on a road. He met a man who was part of the Ethiopian court. Philip's attention was drawn to this man because he was reading from the book of Isaiah, which is in the Old Testament. He was reading a part of Isaiah that seems to speak of Jesus years before Jesus was even born. Philip asked the Ethiopian if he understood what he was reading.

"How can I," the man asked in response, "unless someone explains it to me?"

That might be a good question for us to ask, too. Life is complicated and messy. Sometimes it can be hard to figure out how to apply to our modern-day problems what Jesus wants. We can feel frustrated because it's so hard to figure out all this stuff on our own.

Well, do you know what? Jesus doesn't want us to do that. We don't need to. He gave us leaders—leaders such as bishops, priests, sisters, teachers, writers, and even our own parents—to pass on the Good News, to make sure that it's taught right, and to help us figure out how to find God's love today, in the twenty-first century.

So sure, we're just like that Ethiopian when it comes to nurturing the virtue of prudence. We want to make careful decisions that reflect God's love, but sometimes we need help. How can we know, we wonder, if someone doesn't explain it to us?

Don't worry—there's help. Jesus knew we needed it, and so, through those apostles who listened to him and everyone who listens to them, he gives that help to us so we can listen and make our choices with that really important virtue called prudence helping us all the time.

Paul and Barnabas at Lystra

Heroes See the Good in All Things

We all have bad days. We've all had bad things happen to us. We've all been in situations that were less than great.

Maybe, just once or twice in your life, you've had to take a class from a teacher who wasn't going to win any awards soon, at least not for good teaching. But did you know that it's really hard to teach when a class is out of control? So there you sit in this awful class—bored, entertained by the chaos all around you, or perhaps both. What should you do? You have a lot of choices. You

could join in the fun. You could zone out. You could cross off learning long division this year. You could refuse to even try to make it better for yourself or anyone else.

A tough decision, that's true. Maybe that virtue called prudence might come in handy here. Prudence helps us look at a situation and make the right decision about what to do. It helps us see something amazing but true: that there's good in every situation. Prudence also helps us *do* something amazing but true: it helps us find that spark of good, work with it, and bring even more good out of the situation.

The early Christians lived in a world full of hard, weird, and difficult situations. After all, there were only a few Christians, all of them running around sharing the good news of Jesus' resurrection. There were a whole lot more non-Christians—people who worshipped other gods; people who didn't believe in any god; people who believed in the one, true God, but didn't believe that Jesus was the Messiah; and people who were far less interested in religion than they were in their own pleasures and powers.

But if more people were going to come to know the love of Jesus, the apostles knew that they couldn't let themselves be discouraged by these difficult situations. They knew the people whom they were going to share Jesus' love with had different ideas about the world than they did. These people might even be hostile to the apostles and their preaching. Somewhere, somehow, the apostles had to find the good and use it to bring even more good into situations that often looked pretty bad.

Of all the apostles, Paul was one of the busiest travelers. Now remember that Paul wasn't one of the original twelve apostles called by Jesus during his time on earth. But Paul did receive a very personal call from Jesus as he was on the road to Damascus, and because of that, Paul believed he had the perfect right to be called an apostle.

After his conversion, Paul spent his life traveling. He spread the good news of Jesus' love all around the Middle East and southern Europe—what we now call Greece and Italy.

Paul didn't just drift from place to place, though. He had a plan. When he came to a new village or town, Paul tried to visit the Jewish community first. This made sense because Paul was talking about Jesus, the Messiah the Jewish people had been waiting for.

But sometimes, when the Jewish communities weren't interested in what Paul had to say, or after he had finished his work with them, Paul would talk to pagans—people who worshipped other gods. Sometimes he talked to them without meaning to, which is what happened to him and his companion Barnabas in a town called Lystra.

They were preaching the Gospel, and one of their listeners was a crippled man. Paul noticed what close attention the man was paying to him, and in just a few moments, Paul could see how open this man was to the love of God. Taking a chance, Paul told the man to stand up and walk, and the man did!

Now, when the people of Lystra saw what had happened, they jumped to a very interesting conclusion: Paul and Barnabas must be gods come down to earth.

It's almost funny to think of the scene: Poor Paul and Barnabas had come to share the truth about Jesus but were surrounded by crowds who were convinced that they were really gods called Zeus and Hermes. There was a temple to Zeus outside the city, and even the temple's priest got into the action: he brought garlands of flowers and—get ready for this—some young bulls to sacrifice to Paul and Barnabas.

Not exactly what they had planned, was it?

If you think about it, it's a situation in which Paul had several choices. He could have let the crowd believe their fantasy, take the sacrifice and the honors, and then disappear into the night with a funny story to tell for the rest of his life. Or he could have just run and kept running until he was out of town.

He could have also just tell the truth about himself. That might seem like a simple thing, but it's really not. If you've ever been in an excited crowd, you know how strange that can be. Crowds almost have a life of their own—happiness can turn to anger in seconds. And if the crowd in Lystra learned the truth, there was always the chance that they could feel as if Paul and Barnabas had tried to trick them, and then the crowd might turn on them.

What was the right decision? How could Paul figure out where God was in all of this, and how he could serve God best?

Figuring this out was a good exercise of the virtue of prudence. Paul and Barnabas didn't waste any time. They rushed into the crowd and told the truth. They weren't gods. There was only one God. Paul also tried to help the crowd see hints of the true God's love for them in the workings of nature. He was trying to draw everything good and true out of this scary situation.

As it happens, the ending isn't exactly happy for Paul. The crowd ended up throwing stones at him and dragging him out of the city. But who knows what seeds he planted in Lystra? And what other choice did he have that would have been faithful to God? He had to tell the truth about God, and what's more, he tried to do it in a way that drew the truth from what the people already knew about nature.

Practicing the virtue of prudence, Paul looked at what was going on around him. Sure, there was danger in telling the truth, but what about the alternative? If he didn't tell the truth, the people would never hear the good news about Jesus. And if they didn't tell the truth, the crowd would have had a very good reason to continue believing in their false gods—after all, "Zeus" and "Hermes" had just healed a crippled man before their very eyes.

So, looking at everything, Paul used prudence to make the right choice and to be faithful to Jesus, no matter the risk.

Now back to that wretched class.

This is really hard, it's true. You probably don't feel like being a big prophet and preaching to your classmates about doing the right thing. But is there any good you can find in this chaos? Any good that you can build on?

You may not be able to turn the whole class around, but maybe tomorrow, you can turn one classmate around, and the two of you—or maybe three of you—can refuse to take part in the pranks and instead cooperate with the teacher. Then in a few days, maybe each of you can decide to bring one other person into the cooperative side of the room. And maybe, in a couple of weeks, there will only be a couple of troublemakers left, and they can take a hike down to the principal's office.

God is everywhere—in a group of confused pagans who want to slaughter a bull for you, and even in a difficult classroom. It's up to us to search and find that good, and then make decisions about working with God to build on that good. That's prudence.

St. Jean de Brébeuf

A Hero Respects Others

Every day, everywhere you go, you're faced with choices about how you're going to treat other people.

How will you respond to the girl who, for some unknown reason, has started cutting you down every time she sees you? How will you answer your mom when she asks you to come down into the living room and just spend some time with her, talking? How will you treat the kid who always hangs around your group at recess or after school, looking like he wants to join in, but never saying a word?

Prudence is the virtue that helps us look at situations and make the right decisions. When we practice the virtue of prudence, we're looking for the good in everything and letting God help us draw even more good out. Quite simply, we're letting God guide our actions.

And when we're faced with a choice about how to respond to another person, one of the best places to start is to remember who that person is. Sure, that person might be a classmate, a stranger, or even your mom. But in every case, that person is someone else, too: a child of God.

The saints are people we remember and honor because, among other things, they never forgot that every person they met was their brother or sister. That knowledge guided their actions and led to their prudent decisions about how to treat people.

Hundreds of years ago, travelers journeyed from Europe to North America. They all had different reasons for making the trip. Some wanted more land for their countries. Others—many, in fact—had heard stories about the great wealth available in the New World, and they wanted to get as much of it as they could.

But there were others, as well. Men, and later women, came to the wild new land because they had heard that there were people already living in this land. These people—the Native Americans living from Canada down to South America—were of many nations, some peaceful, some warlike, some wandering, and some settled. But none of them had heard of Jesus. They were God's children, though, and they deserved to hear the Good News. So, from across the sea, men and women came to share it with them.

These priests, brothers, and sisters left comfortable lives in Europe to come to a strange land that was often very dangerous. Sometimes these religious men and women treated some of the indigenous peoples badly, but most of the time, they tried to care for them with respect. One of those who had the deepest respect for the indigenous peoples, and who left records to show it, was St. Jean de Brébeuf.

St. Jean was a Jesuit priest who made his first journey to Canada in 1625. The tribe to which he devoted most of his energy was the Huron tribe. He lived with the Hurons for most of the rest of his life. He learned their language, even though it was very difficult. He cared for them, tried to teach them about Jesus, and encouraged them to be baptized.

There were many problems, of course. First of all, the living conditions were very difficult. Fr. Brébeuf was a sickly man and the way he had to live didn't help his health. He lived with the Hurons in their dark, airless dwellings. He ate their food, which didn't exactly taste great to him.

Second, Fr. Brébeuf also had to live with the Huron's superstitions. The Hurons were very suspicious of the European priests, whom they called Black Robes. If the weather was fine, the crops were good, and the villagers were healthy, there was no problem. But if drought struck, or crops failed, or a fever swept through the village, life got dangerous for the priests. The Hurons were afraid that the gods and spirits were punishing them for allowing the priests to live among them and baptize them. Because of this, the priests were always in danger of being driven away from the village, or worse.

Finally, danger always lurked from the outside. Native American tribes in Canada were constantly at war during this time, and the battles were often made worse by the conflicts between the French and the English. The Huron tribe was under particular threat from the Iroquois. War is never clean or polite, and many tribes were cruel to those they conquered.

St. Jean de Brébeuf had traveled a long way to live with and teach people who had never heard of Jesus. He could have chosen to treat them with disrespect, as did many Europeans. He could have forced them into baptism. He could have tried to use their superstitions to his advantage. He could have tried to scare them. He could have asked French soldiers to help force the Hurons into becoming Christian.

But he didn't. Guided by prudence, looking at what God wanted him to do in the situation, he made the choice to love the Hurons and live with them, sharing the Good News patiently and kindly. We know he did this because he left records. He wrote to other priests who were coming to America to tell them what they should expect and how they should treat the indigenous peoples.

He wrote to the Europeans of the dangers of his life, saying "You may expect to be killed at any moment. . . . You are responsible for the weather, be it foul or fair, and if you don't bring rain when it's needed you may be tomahawked for your lack of luck."

St. Jean also told future missionaries how to behave when traveling with the Native Americans. This was important, because missionaries would do a lot of traveling when they arrived, and they couldn't do it on their own—they needed the indigenous peoples to guide them.

So, St. Jean wrote that the missionaries should never keep the Native Americans waiting when it was time to go. They should not be troublesome or ask many questions. Most of the trip would be taken by canoe on rivers and lakes, but there were times when that would be impossible, and the canoes and supplies would have to be carried. St. Jean tells the missionaries that they should always carry their fair share during these times.

He also reminds them that when the journey is made on the water, they should not even start to paddle unless they are going to keep it up at the same pace as their guides. Don't complain, St. Jean says, and always be cheerful.

And most important, St. Jean begins his rules with the very strong reminder: "You must love these Hurons, ransomed by the blood of the Son of God, as brothers."

Jean de Brébeuf lived a hard life, and he had to make wise decisions. He had to decide the best way to help the Native Americans and share the love of Jesus with them. He made his decision—to treat the Hurons respectfully and lovingly—by listening to them and by listening to God in his heart.

When we decide how to treat others, we should practice the virtue of prudence, too. We should act wisely, seeing others with the loving eyes of God and listening to our conscience. We can have all kinds of reasons for treating others the way we do: we want to prove something, we don't want them to win an argument, we don't want to look dumb or weak or uncool. But are any of those really good reasons? Letting prudence guide us, instead of fear or anger, will show us the answer, just as it showed Jean de Brébeuf:

"You must love . . . as brothers."

Catherine Doherty and St. Laura Montoya Upegui

Heroes Bring New Ideas

In the old days, it was all so easy. You would do something wrong—scribble on the wall with a crayon, pull the cat's tail, dump your bowl of cereal out because a milk river would look so cool running across the table—and what would happen? A little bit of yelling, maybe a tap on the hand, maybe a time-out . . . but with a simple little "I'm sorry" from you, it was over. Apology accepted, no further explanation needed.

But things seem to have changed. Your parents aren't satisfied with just "I'm sorry" anymore. They want to know *why* you did whatever you did. They look all worried, like you've put yourself on the path to prison or something. And even the punishments are changing—they're obviously trying to get you to think about what you did.

Life changes, there's no doubt about it. And believe it or not, we usually have to do some changing along with it. Sometimes the old ways just don't work, and we have to figure out a new way of making good choices, being ourselves, and being happy about it all. We can't be stuck in the past. We have to be brave and be willing to do something new. It's just one more way of practicing that virtue of prudence: making wise decisions without being afraid of what new things may come out of them.

There are countless stories we could tell about the importance of prudence, but here we'll tell just two, about two women, one Russian and the other Colombian, who each saw that the world needed new answers to old problems. They answered God's call to bring his love to all sorts of people in new ways: to people of different races, to the poor, and to the rejected and ignored.

The Russian woman was named Catherine de Hueck Doherty. She was born in 1896 in Nizhniy-Novgorod, Russia. Catherine's family was very religious, and her parents were both deeply dedicated to helping the poor. When Catherine was a girl, her father had to take a job in Egypt. Catherine was enrolled in a Catholic school there. The story is told that one day, Catherine saw a very realistic crucifix in one of her classrooms, and she was so moved by the sight of the suffering Jesus that she ran and got a washcloth and soap and tried to cleanse Jesus' wounds of blood.

In a way, that scene tells the story of the rest of Catherine's life. Everywhere she went throughout the world, she saw suffering (and if you look, you will see it, too), and in those suffering people, she saw Jesus. How could she turn from that suffering without trying to help?

During World War I (1914 to 1918), Catherine served as a nurse in the Russian army. After the war, Russia underwent a revolution in which Communists took over the government and persecuted many people. Catherine escaped, first to England, and then to Canada, but work was hard to come by.

Catherine then moved to New York, where she was able to get a good job working with books and giving speeches. While she lived in New York, Catherine noticed with great sadness how people of different races sometimes had a hard time getting along. It was a deep hurt in the human family, which meant it was hurting Jesus. Catherine saw what was happening and listened to God's voice in her conscience. That voice was calling her to jump right in and do something. When we look at situations and make wise, brave decisions, we're being prudent, and that's what Catherine was being.

Reading, studying, and praying over the life of Jesus, Catherine saw that there was really nothing more important in life than trying to be like Jesus. Part of that meant living a life like Jesus did: a life of simplicity. So Catherine and her husband, Eddie Doherty, moved to a rural part of Ontario, Canada, where they built a home and dedicated their lives to prayer and very simple living. Much to her surprise, Catherine started having visitors: people who had heard about her simple, Jesus-centered way of life at what she called "Madonna House" and wanted to share it.

Catherine's Madonna House would be many things. It would be a place where people who wanted to give their lives to Jesus could come and stay after they had sold their possessions and left their lives in the world. It would be a place for people to come and pray in peace. It would also be a place where poor people could come for help.

Again, what Catherine saw was the need for something new. Even during this time—the 1940s and 1950s—the world was becoming a very busy place. It was even a dangerous place. Catherine saw that people were in danger of getting too busy and getting too interested in making money. Madonna House was an answer. It was place for people to go when they found that the old way of doing things—the busyness and the fear—was keeping them away from God. Madonna House was a sign that if you chose a new way of doing things, you could be happy.

Catherine died in 1985, but there are still Madonna Houses around the world today, showing people what can happen when you practice the virtue of prudence, look at a situation that needs help, and make a wise, courageous choice to make it better.

Laura Montoya Upegui came into the world a few years before Catherine, far away from Russia. She was born in 1874 in Colombia in South America. Since her family was quite poor, she worked to support herself and help her mother. Laura was smart and wanted to use her talents to help others, so she went to school to learn to be a teacher.

How would Laura use her gifts and her training? She had some choices to make. She could teach in a regular school for girls in the capital city of Medellín, or she could return to her hometown and work there. She could even join a convent, and at times Laura's heart felt strongly pulled to that quiet life. She could see herself setting aside teaching and devoting her life to God in prayer, day and night. What would she do?

Laura used the gift of prudence. She prayed, she looked around her, and she listened. And what did she see and hear? People suffering. Laura couldn't ignore it, and she especially couldn't ignore the suffering of a special group—the indigenous peoples of Colombia. They had been living in the mountains and jungles, and by the rivers of the land, long before explorers and conquerors had arrived from Europe. Now, hundreds of years later, the indigenous peoples were the poorest of all those dwelling in Colombia. They had the least access to education, and they received the least respect in society.

Who needed to know the love of Jesus more? So into the jungle plunged Laura. Other women joined her, and together they worked to help the indigenous peoples in ways that no one else thought necessary or even possible. They taught them how to read and write, they taught them modern skills, but most importantly, they taught them about God's love. And they taught them, not just with words, but by actions. They lived with them, adopted their traditional ways, and spoke their languages. There was no doubt: Laura and her friends were their sisters and friends.

Many people back in the cities looked down on how Laura and her friends lived with the indigenous peoples. They called them "wild beasts" and thought they should be forced to give up their traditions and culture. But Laura, using the gift of prudence, saw differently. She saw the goodness in those communities and their traditional ways. Opening herself to God's courage, St. Laura started a community that still serves today in many countries. These religious sisters help and love just as St. Laura did, remembering how Jesus shared his light: not by keeping himself above the world, but by coming right into it and walking with us, just as we are.

So it's true. The old ways may be comfortable for many of us for a while, but sooner or later, those old ways wear out or even start hurting people. When we grow out of our old ways, we can start seeing and doing more. God wants us all to be looking at his world with open eyes and thinking prudently: We see what works and what doesn't, and then we have the courage and creativity to do something new!

Blessed Solanus Casey

A Hero Accepts His Life

You really wanted to make the team—and what's more, you thought you had a pretty good chance, too. But the coach didn't seem to agree since your name isn't on the final roster.

Wow. You had imagined how your life would be this fall, and you thought your talents would take you there. But others didn't see it the same way, and you're left with an unexpected amount of free time over the next few months, not to mention a lot of energy and some hurt feelings.

What do you do now?

That's going to take some thinking, isn't it? You're going to have to look at the situation, think about your talents all over again, and maybe even listen to God in prayer. He knows what's up. He knows what to do.

You're going to have to haul out that virtue we call prudence—looking at a situation and making wise decisions about it—and use it to figure things out.

It's frustrating to feel a really strong desire or call to use your talents in a certain way, but then be rejected. This kind of disappointment happens more than you know. It even happens to saints and other holy people. And it happens a lot. Maybe we can figure out what to do with that kind of disappointment in our own lives if we look at what they did.

Solanus Casey knew all about frustration. His deepest desire was to serve God as a priest—but his religious superiors didn't really think he was smart enough. But the story of Blessed Solanus Casey shows very clearly that God can do his work despite our weaknesses and those of the people who decide what to do with us!

Bernard Casey was born in Wisconsin in 1870 to a huge family—he had thirteen brothers and sisters! Like the rest of his family, Bernard spent his childhood working on the farm. He moved to a city when he got to be a teenager, worked in various jobs, and dated girls.

But all along, something in Bernard's heart was calling him to be deeper friends with God. This feeling became a decision when one terrible day, Bernard, who was working as a streetcar conductor, had to bring the streetcar he was controlling to a screeching halt—standing right in the middle of the road was a man with a knife in his hand, standing over the body of the woman he had just murdered. It was a horrible scene, and it showed Bernard how badly people needed God's love and peace. He felt a call to serve, and so he answered it.

So, Bernard thought he knew what God wanted. You'd think everything would go smoothly now—but it didn't. He tried to study for the priesthood in two different schools, but in both he had the same problem. The lessons were in German and Latin, and he didn't speak or read either language very well. Bernard had a really hard time in school.

He was asked to leave the first school, but the second, run by a religious order called the Capuchins, which is a kind of Franciscan order, gave him a chance even though he was one of the worst students they had. Along with that chance, though, they gave him some conditions.

Bernard's superiors in the Capuchins saw that Bernard was a man of prayer, but he was a truly awful student. They decided to let him continue, but on one condition: He had to sign a piece of paper saying that he would accept any decision they made about him. That is, he could continue as a Capuchin brother, but they wouldn't promise that he would be ordained a priest—the goal of all of his hard schoolwork in the first place!

Bernard agreed because he couldn't deny the call of God. He had thought the call was to serve as a priest, but maybe he was wrong. He would just wait and see.

It was actually pretty humiliating, if you think about it, but Bernard—who now took the name Solanus after the great Franciscan missionary St. Francis Solanus—didn't get discouraged. He knew that God wanted him to serve him, and he would just wait for a sign of how that would happen.

As it turned out, the Capuchins did allow Solanus to be ordained, but he would be a special kind of priest called a simplex priest. He would be able to do everything a priest could do except hear confessions and preach a formal sermon at Mass. His superiors just didn't trust that he understood enough of his studies to tell other people about the faith.

Again, Solanus could have been angry and humiliated, but he wasn't. He just kept waiting for his chance to serve. And it came when Fr. Solanus got his first assignment at a parish in New York.

Now since Fr. Solanus couldn't hear confessions or preach, they had to find a job for him. First, they gave him the job of training altar servers (which was usually given to a deacon) and then the job of porter (which was usually given to a brother, not a priest).

A porter is the person who sits at the door of a monastery and greets people—sort of like a receptionist. Fr. Solanus's job was to sort the mail, take telephone calls, and greet visitors. Since poor people often come to churches for help, directing them to the help they need is also a big part of the porter's job.

Little did anyone know what else would become a part of *this* porter's job.

Very quickly, Fr. Solanus Casey became known in the neighborhood as a very holy man. All kinds of people started coming to him with their problems. He listened carefully and prayed with the people. He told them to trust in God. And within a short time, amazing things started happening.

Sick people for whom Fr. Solanus had prayed started getting well. Families for whom Fr. Solanus had prayed started getting along better. And sometimes, Fr. Solanus was even able to tell people what would happen in the future. On a visit to a hospital, he met a person worried about a sick child. He assured the parent that the child would recover. He did. On the next floor, he met a man whose wife had just undergone minor surgery. He told the man to prepare to give his wife to God. She died two days later.

Fr. Solanus served as the porter in every Capuchin church where he lived: in New York, Detroit, and Indiana. He sat at a desk near the door, greeting, smiling, and praying. One of the other Capuchins estimated that between 150 and 200 people would come to Fr. Solanus every day. Most of them just asked for a simple blessing, but Fr. Solanus found the time to seriously listen to as many as fifty a day.

Even on his deathbed in 1957, at the age of eighty-seven, Fr. Solanus found time to help. A woman who had lost two babies during pregnancy heard he was in the hospital where she was visiting her mother. She asked permission to see him. She told the weak, frail Fr. Solanus of her troubles and asked him to pray for her that she might have a healthy baby. He assured her that she would—and five years later, this grateful woman gave birth to twins.

Fr. Solanus died a few days later, after a long life of loving God and serving people. He died on the same day and at the same hour he had said his first Mass, fifty-three years before.

It's kind of funny the way God finds a way around our limited view of things. Fr. Solanus's superiors were afraid he would give bad advice in confessions because he was a bad student, but God ended up using him to listen to people anyway. Day in and day out, he shared the good news of God's love with them!

Throughout his life, Blessed Solanus Casey could have become discouraged and angry that his gifts and talents weren't recognized by those who were making decisions about him. He could have made quick, bad decisions based on how he felt. He could have left the Franciscans. He could have lived in anger and taken it out on others.

But he didn't do any of that. He accepted life as it was and kept on praying, knowing that God had a plan for him, and that if he listened carefully and acted with prudence, he would find out what that plan was.

St. John XXIII

A Hero Finds a New Way

You thought it would be a happy birthday, but you never thought it would be quite *this* happy. Between three grandparents, one godparent, an aunt, and a lazy big brother, your wallet has suddenly grown about seventy dollars fatter. So, what are you going to do with your wealth?

Let's see. You could go out and spend it all this afternoon. You might be able to get one new and one used video game with that kind of money. That sounds like a great idea until you remember last year. You saved a bunch of money, spent it all on a game you'd been wanting for a long time, then played through

the game and beat it in two days. It was kind of fun, but really—all that money for just two days of entertainment?

Here's something else to consider, besides your past experiences. How about the future? In just a few weeks, your family is going to be taking a big trip out West, and who knows what cool stuff you might find along the way?

Sounds good. But then one more thing pops into your head—the present. More specifically, what Jesus is saying to you right this minute about that cash. What does he want you to do with that money, anyway?

Making decisions is tough. There's a lot to consider. You have to think about what the past has taught you. You need to keep the future in mind. And above all, you need to consider what your best friend, Jesus, has to say about it all to you right this minute, in the present. After all, he does know best.

Taking the past, future, and God's will in the present into account when you make a decision is really important. It's more than important—it's one more way of living out that virtue called prudence.

You can see that being prudent is important in making decisions for yourself. It's even more important when you're given the responsibility of making decisions that are going to affect a lot of people. That's why prudence is such a good virtue for leaders to have.

The twentieth century was an amazing century. Life changed dramatically during those years, mostly for the good. Diseases like polio and smallpox were conquered. People could travel across the world in a day on airplanes and communicate with each other in seconds on the Internet and the telephone.

But not everything was great in the twentieth century. It was a century filled with horrible wars that killed millions and with evil leaders—like Stalin in Russia, Mao in China, and Hitler in Germany—who slaughtered tens of millions of people, too. Technology brought us wonderful inventions that made life easier and more fun, but it also brought us weapons that could wipe out half the earth, if they were ever used.

With so much possibility for good and evil, the twentieth century was a time that needed good leaders who could look at the past, present, and future and make good, prudent decisions. Even the church needed leaders like that. Just when we needed it most, God gave us a gift: Pope John XXIII, who was pope for only a short time (1959 to 1963) but who had an amazing impact on the church and the entire world.

Of course, John XXIII was not the name he was born with. His parents named him Angelo—Angelo Roncalli, born in 1881 in the northern part of Italy. His family farmed for a living, and Angelo was the oldest boy of twelve brothers and sisters.

Angelo's earliest memories are of his mother at prayer. He could remember trotting alongside his mother, who was carrying two babies and pregnant with another—on a long walk through the country that ended up at a beautiful shrine dedicated to Mary.

When he was a teenager, Angelo decided he wanted to be a priest. He studied in the seminary, where he was most interested in the history of the church. After he was ordained a priest, Angelo expected nothing more out of the rest of his life than that of a normal parish priest back in the part of Italy where he'd grown up. It was what he knew and what he thought God was calling him to. But very soon, it became clear that God had other plans for Angelo.

Over the course of his career, Fr. Angelo held many jobs, some exciting, some difficult. He was a secretary to a bishop for ten years. He served as a medical worker in battlefields during World War I, and he never forgot the suffering he witnessed there. He represented the church in countries like Bulgaria and Turkey, countries where there were hardly any Catholics, and it was really important to understand and get along with people of different religions.

Finally, when he was seventy-one years old, Fr. Angelo Roncalli came home. He was appointed to be the leader of the church in the city of Venice, Italy. Fr. Angelo—now archbishop—had come home and, for all he knew, would spend the rest of his life simply tending to the needs of the people of Venice.

But once again, God had something else in mind. In 1958, Pope Pius XII died, and, as always happens when a pope dies, all the cardinals of the church gathered to elect a replacement. Much to everyone's surprise, they elected Angelo Roncalli of Venice. He was seventy-six years old.

Now, you would think that a seventy-six-year-old man would know his place. You'd think he would settle into the Vatican, sit comfortably in his chair, and just hold the fort until God called him home and a younger, more energetic man could get things going.

Not quite. Angelo—who was now Pope John XXIII—had plenty of energy and plenty of ideas. The time for action was now. The Spirit was calling, and Pope John XXIII, thinking of the past, present, and future, was going to answer.

First of all, John XXIII knew that times had changed, and it was time for popes to stop acting like royalty, which they had been doing for too many years. John was supposed to wear a big, jeweled tiara on his head. He wore it twice. When he went from place to place, he was supposed to sit in a special chair that would be hoisted up onto the shoulders of men who would then carry him. Even though John was a large man and being carried would have been easier than walking, he usually preferred to walk.

Reporters had to interview the previous pope while on their knees in front of him. John stopped that right away. He was the bishop of Rome, so he acted like it, going into the city of Rome and mingling with people. The very first Christmas he was pope, John visited two children's hospitals in Rome, spending time with sick children, something that people could remember no other pope doing before.

John knew that the Spirit had called him to serve the people of God, not to act like a prince among them. But that wasn't the only thing he knew had to change.

When John XXIII was elected pope, the world was a very different place than it had been even two hundred years before. In the past, the church had a lot of power in the world. That wasn't the case anymore. Nations had much more power than the church and were sometimes using that power to hurt people. John believed that the church needed to speak with a stronger voice so that it could protect all people from war, violence, and poverty.

Other things had changed, too. There were new ways of thinking about the world, ways that had nothing to do with religion or the Bible. Many people had come to believe that the advances of science made faith in God unnecessary. John saw much good in new scientific discoveries, but he also knew that without God we are lost. He wanted to help people who had faith learn how to talk to people who did not have faith in ways they could understand and in ways that would help everyone see the truth of God's love.

In other words, what John XXIII wanted was to open the church up to the world so that the church could spread the good news of Jesus' love in a way that made sense to people of the new century. It wasn't the Middle Ages anymore. It was the twentieth century. John wanted the whole world to be able to hear the Good News in twentieth-century words.

So John looked to the past. He saw that the while the church had always preached the same Gospel, the way it had been preached over the years changed from time to time. Change was okay, and nothing to be afraid of.

He looked to the future. He saw that the world needed Jesus very badly, and if the church didn't try to understand modern times, lots of people might never hear about Jesus.

And John XXIII listened to the Spirit in the present. He listened to God speaking in his heart, looked at the responsibility he'd been given, and answered that voice.

He called an ecumenical council—what we call the Second Vatican Council. During this council, all the bishops of the world gathered in Rome for three years (1962 to 1965). They prayed, discussed, and studied. They wrote many papers outlining new, exciting ways the church could spread the old, unchanging truth about God's love in the modern world. The church you see today preaches the same Good News it always has, but in a way that's very different today than it was before the council, and that's because these are different times.

John XXIII had a vision and hope. He made a decision based on that hope and based on the virtue of prudence, a virtue that he spoke of a great deal. John—whom today we call St. John XXIII—believed that Jesus' love was for everybody in the world.

He wanted the church to be a strong voice proclaiming that love in modern times to modern people. He looked to the past, present, and future in making his decision to lead the church in that direction.

When we make prudent decisions, that's exactly what we have to do, too: We should think about the past, understand how our choice will affect us in the future, and listen to God's voice in our hearts in the present.

Popes and kids—we're all called to be prudent. We're all called to be wise!

Fortitude

The Lord is my strength.

Psalm 118:14

Jesus Is Crucified

There are lots of ways to be strong.

You can develop your muscles and learn to lift big, heavy weights. You can go out every day and practice running until you can go several miles without stopping. You can spend a couple of hours a day on the tennis court until no one—not even your dad—can return your mighty serve.

Or you can set your sights on what's good and true, and decide to live by that, no matter what. That's a kind of strength, too. It's a strength of character and spirit. You might even say it's the most important kind of strength. When we talk about the strength to do good and be faithful to God no matter what, we even have a special name for it: It's called fortitude.

Fortitude is a really important virtue because you know how difficult it is to be faithful to your friendship with God. There are just so many temptations to turn away and take what seems like an easier road.

Since God knows everything, he knows this, too. He knows how weak we are, so he's always with us, ready to build up our fortitude with his love and grace. He's also given us the best example of fortitude we could ever want or need: Jesus, suffering and crucified.

Jesus had been teaching, healing, and caring for the people in Palestine for around three years. Wherever he went, he drew crowds. Some in the crowds were curious. Some needed help and healing. And some, unfortunately, came to see if they could catch Jesus doing something wrong.

For you see, not everyone was happy with what Jesus was doing and saying. Religious leaders were puzzled by him. He talked a lot about God, but there were certain rules of the Jewish faith that he didn't seem to care much about—he disobeyed the rule about working on the Sabbath, for example, by letting his disciples pick corn on that day and by performing a healing.

Jesus also did things that, when you think about it, only God can do. The most important of these was forgiving sins. Sure, I can forgive you for the sins you've committed against me, but wouldn't you think it was strange if I said to you, "Go, your sins are forgiven"? Wouldn't you think that only God has the power to say things like that? Well, you'd be right. And that worried some religious leaders. Who did Jesus think he was?

Finally, Jesus had some hard words to say about some religious leaders. He often said that they said one thing and did another. He accused them of telling people that they had to live a certain way in order to be pleasing to God, and then failing to live that way themselves. None of this made religious leaders happy.

The Roman leaders of the people of Palestine weren't happy with Jesus, either. He was drawing crowds, which wasn't a good thing because you know how messy crowds can get. People were also calling him the Messiah, which the Roman leaders understood to mean the new king of the Jewish people. They worried that this Jesus might start a revolution against their power.

In the end, during one terrible week, all of these worries came together, and thanks to the betrayal of the apostle Judas, Jesus was arrested by the Roman authorities.

You know the story, but it really is worth thinking about again and again. Jesus was an innocent man. He came to share God's love with the world. He had strong words for some, but it was all in the name of truth and love.

Jesus was also Lord. He did not have to submit to these powers that arrested him. At the very beginning of his ministry, Satan tempted Jesus to come out and use his powers to make the world into his servant, right then and there.

Jesus could have. But he didn't. Because he loved us, he took up his cross and carried it. Because he loved us, he suffered on that cross and died.

Because he loved us.

> Those who passed by derided him, shaking their heads and saying, "Aha! You who would destroy the temple and build it in three days, save yourself, and come down from the cross!" In the same way the chief priests, along with the scribes, were also mocking him

among themselves and saying, "He saved others; he cannot save himself. Let the Messiah, the King of Israel, come down from the cross now, so that we may see and believe." Those who were crucified with him also taunted him.

When it was noon, darkness came over the whole land until three in the afternoon. At three o'clock Jesus cried out with a loud voice, "Eloi, Eloi, lema sabachthani?" which means, "My God, my God, why have you forsaken me?" When some of the bystanders heard it, they said, "Listen, he is calling for Elijah." And someone ran, filled a sponge with sour wine, put it on a stick, and gave it to him to drink, saying, "Wait, let us see whether Elijah will come to take him down." Then Jesus gave a loud cry and breathed his last. And the curtain of the temple was torn in two, from top to bottom. Now when the centurion, who stood facing him, saw that in this way he breathed his last, he said, "Truly this man was God's Son!" (Mark 15:29–39)

That's why many of us have crucifixes in our homes and around our necks. The sight of Jesus on the cross is a sign of love and a sign of strength. It doesn't take any strength to give into evil, does it? In fact, that is the very definition of weakness.

No, we want to be strong for Jesus, strong for the truth, and strong for love. We don't want evil to be victorious in any part of our lives. So we hold on to fortitude, remember Jesus on the cross, and stay strong for the sake of love.

St. Stephen

A Hero Stays Strong in Faith

Until just a few weeks ago, all the kids in your class had been getting along just fine. Sure, there were spats and hurt feelings sometimes, but in general, things were pretty great.

Until this one girl—a friend of yours, by the way—started getting all obsessed and weird about being "popular." She's even going around telling people whether they're popular or not and explaining why.

It's very strange, and it's hurting the class. You're losing that family feeling, and people are starting to get sucked in and judge each other. Is there anything you can do? Maybe, but before you

can even get to entering that battle and making sure more people don't get hurt, you've got to conquer something inside you—fear.

There's a lot to be afraid of in this situation. You might be afraid of being shut out, of being thought of as a goody-goody, of being called something even worse than unpopular.

But you can do it. With God's help you can conquer that fear and make a choice to act with strength. You can take a deep breath and remember that when you're committed to that virtue of fortitude, God will get you through and make you strong.

The early apostles knew all about fortitude. They knew that Jesus was their model for strength. If they imitated him and were strong despite their fear, they would be given the gift of resurrection.

This came in handy, of course, because almost all of the apostles and early close disciples of Jesus ended up following the exact path he did: giving their life for God's truth and love. The first we know about was Stephen.

Stephen wasn't one of the original twelve apostles, but he was close! As you remember, the Christian church began in Jerusalem, the city where Jesus had been crucified and rose from the dead. The Christian community in Jerusalem was filled with the love of Jesus and very busy. They were committed to helping the poor, and to do this in an organized way, they selected some men to serve as deacons. Stephen was one of these first deacons.

He may have been one of several, but very quickly, Stephen began to stand out from the rest of the group. The Acts of the Apostles, the book in the Bible that relates the story of the early church, tells us that Stephen became known as a worker of "wonders and signs." This means that God worked through him to heal.

Stephen could also explain faith in Jesus very clearly. Other religious leaders would come and try to argue with him, but Stephen always came out on top, making the truth clear to everyone: Jesus had risen and was Lord.

You probably won't be surprised to hear that at last, some religious leaders grew very angry with Stephen and wanted to stop him from acting and speaking. So they found people who would lie and say that Stephen was speaking against the Jewish temple and the Jewish Law. In that time and place, that was enough to get him arrested and put on trial by the religious leaders.

Now, at this point, Stephen could have made a choice. He could have stepped back and tried to get out of the way of what was coming. He could have decided that the truth wasn't worth any hardship to him. He could have given into fear and given up on the truth.

But he didn't. Stephen was amazingly strong. Acts tells us that Stephen had so much fortitude that he was able to stand up and make a very long speech during his trial. In this speech, Stephen spoke even more strongly for Jesus. He went through the stories in the Old Testament and showed the leaders how too many times in the past, the people had refused to listen to God. He said that this was one of those times. Jesus had risen from the dead. It was clear that he was the Messiah, that he was Lord. If the leaders didn't listen to this, they would be turning from the truth that God was giving them.

Not exactly a cowardly speech. No, it was a speech full of the truth and full of strength.

Of course, the ending to this story seems scary and sad. The leaders refused to just sit back and be told that they were not listening to God. So they took Stephen outside the court, put him in a large pit in the ground, and gave him the punishment that anyone who spoke like him would receive: they stoned him to death.

These aren't pebbles we're talking about. These are big, heavy rocks, thrown at a defenseless man trapped in a pit. Stephen stayed strong through it all, though. He remembered how Jesus had died, and he tried his best to die the same way. He prayed that God would forgive those who were hurting him. Right before he died, like Jesus, he asked God to receive his spirit.

Stephen may have been the first to die for the truth of God's love in this way, but he wasn't the last. Ancient stories tell us that all of the apostles except John (who died of old age while imprisoned on an island) died violent deaths from those who didn't like what they were saying and doing.

So many friends of Jesus have had so much strength. They could have just walked away from Jesus, gone back to their towns and villages, and lived quiet lives. But that same friendship with Jesus gave them fortitude to endure suffering for the good—and the same Jesus is waiting to help you in just the same way, wherever and whenever you need it!

EGERIA

A Hero Takes a Journey

Friendships are wonderful, but they're not always easy. Lots of things can get in the way. Busy schedules, different interests, and other people's meanness can hurt a friendship. Selfishness can hurt, too, in a lot of ways, including these:

You always go to her house and never yours. You always laugh at his jokes, but because he talks so much, you never get to tell any of your own. You always do things her way.

You might wonder sometimes: Does this kid who says she's my friend even know who I am inside? Does she even care about me? How can she if she never asks?

Our friendship with God—our faith—can be like that, just a little bit. It's not that God isn't interested in us. No way. The problem goes the other way. Sometimes we fall down on our end of the friendship. We talk and talk to God, but we can't take a minute to listen. We tell God all about our lives, but we don't take any time to learn more about God.

A one-sided friendship between you and another kid isn't a very deep or satisfying thing. A one-sided friendship with God is the same way. If we want to be good friends with God, we really need to get to know who he is—and that takes time. And since there are so many other tempting ways to spend our time, it also takes fortitude, strength.

Strength to decide to spend fifteen minutes with a Bible, instead of with a video game. Strength to turn off all the noise in your life and just be quiet and listen. Strength to decide to pay attention at Mass instead of studying other people's clothes.

But at least you're only trying to get the energy to open up a Bible. Do you think you could travel across a continent, mostly on foot, to get to know Jesus better? Would it be worth it?

Hundreds of years ago, a woman named Egeria took a trip like that—she traveled from Spain all the way across Europe over to the Holy Land. Why did she do this? She loved Jesus and was friends with Jesus. She read about Jesus all the time in the Bible. But she wanted to know him even better. She wanted to walk the land where he had walked and breathe the same air. She wanted to give life to the Bible stories she'd read.

We don't know much about Egeria except for the fact that she lived, she took this trip, and she wrote about it. She was a nun, and we know about the trip because she wrote long letters describing her journeys to her sisters in Spain. These letters are about her trip, but they also tell us about this lady: they tell us that she was smart, curious, best friends with Jesus, and that she was very, very strong.

Egeria probably took her trip between the years 381 and 384. This was hundreds and hundreds of years before airplanes and trains were invented. Egeria probably made most of her trip on foot or by boat. She might have ridden in a wagon or on the back of a donkey sometimes, but that probably didn't happen very often. In fact, if she had the choice, Egeria might have turned down the chance for a ride and decided to walk instead. That's because this trip she was taking was a special kind of trip—a pilgrimage.

A pilgrimage is a trip we take to a sacred place with the hopes of becoming closer friends with Jesus. There are two important parts to a pilgrimage. One part is the destination—the holy place you're going to. The second part is the trip itself. Christians like Egeria who are taking these special trips to see the places that Jesus walked, taught, and suffered don't want their trips to be easy or like relaxing vacations. They want to follow in Jesus' footsteps, which means not only seeing what he saw but also feeling what he felt. So why take an easy ride on a wagon over the rough paths on which Jesus walked?

We can be sure that Egeria, like all pilgrims, was ready for hardships on her trip. She didn't mind them. We can see this clearly when we read what Egeria wrote about climbing Mount Sinai.

You probably remember that Mount Sinai was the place where God gave Moses the Ten Commandments. Mount Sinai is a very high mountain in the desert south of Israel. You can climb some mountains by going in circles around it until you reach the top. Mount Sinai wasn't like that—you had to climb straight up and walk straight down. It was dry, rocky, and dangerous. But that didn't stop Egeria. She loved God and her faith and wanted to stand in the same places she believed God had spoken to Moses. She wrote: "It was quite impossible to ride up, but though I had to go on foot, I was not conscious of the effort—in fact I hardly noticed it because, by God's will, I was seeing my hopes coming true."

Egeria traveled all over the Holy Land. She went to Bethlehem where Jesus was born. She went to Galilee and Capernaum, the areas where Jesus grew up and where he kept his home as an adult, on the shores of the Sea of Galilee. She went even farther north, up to Mesopotamia, where Abraham and his family had lived.

At every stop, Egeria tells us, she and her companions explored the place they had come to, read the Bible stories that had occurred there—for example, on the shores of the Jordan River, they read about John baptizing Jesus—and they prayed. You can see this was more than a sightseeing tour!

Jerusalem was Egeria's home base in all of these travels, and in all, she spent over three years there. Jerusalem is the city where Jesus preached, was crucified, and rose from the dead. Egeria attended many religious services while she was there, of course, and she wrote about them in great detail. Because of Egeria, we can see how Christians worshiped sixteen hundred years ago!

And do you know what? The way they worshiped is amazingly like what we do today. Because Jerusalem was then a small city, there was only one church, and that was where the Christians of the city gathered to pray every day. Yes—every day. Christians came to pray in the morning, in the evening, and several times in between.

So much of what Egeria described would sound familiar to you. On Palm Sunday, the Christians of Jerusalem processed through the streets with palm branches. On Holy Thursday, they gathered at the Garden of Gethsemane and followed Jesus' footsteps. On Good Friday, they gathered to give honor to the cross, just as we do in our Good Friday services.

There's no doubt that Egeria was a very brave, strong woman. In those days, travel was dangerous for everyone, and especially for women. You just never knew who was waiting around the next bend in the road, maybe ready to rob you and leave you for dead. There were no hotels, motels, or restaurants. Egeria probably spent most of her nights under the open sky or in tents, eating dried fruit and grain. It was, no doubt, a hard trip. It was a hard trip across the sea, it was hard trip up the mountain, and it was a hard trip through the Holy Land.

But Egeria was a woman of fortitude. She knew what was right and good, and her friendship with God gave her the strength to get where she felt God wanted her to be.

Hard things in life are like the mountain that Egeria climbed, aren't they? We have to work hard to climb them, but knowing the good place we're going makes it seem easy.

When you want to be friends with another person, you sometimes must turn from the temptation to be selfish in that friendship. You have to forget about your own problems and take time to listen to theirs. When you love Jesus, getting to know him better may be a challenge that takes fortitude to meet. It takes strength to turn away from things that give you easy entertainment and quick satisfaction and toward the quieter, slower pace of a good friendship with God.

But fortitude might be easier to hold onto if we, like Egeria, keep our eye on our destination!

Cathedral Builders

Heroes at Work

When you love someone, of course you want to make sure that everything you do for that person is as beautiful as it can be. You think carefully and try to pick out the perfect birthday gift for your best friend. You take time to create a colorful, fun card for your parents' wedding anniversary. And that favorite teacher who actually makes school fun? No mere store-bought Christmas trinket will do for her. You're going to whip up nothing less than a flawless batch of your world-famous chocolate-peanut-crunch-marshmallow bars in appreciation for all she's done.

Since we love God most of all, we want to give the absolute best to him. He's given us life, he's given us love, so of course we want to show how much we appreciate those gifts.

We do that in a lot of ways. The most important way we show our gratitude to God is by following him. We obey the Ten Commandments. We treat people the way Jesus treated them. We let God, not selfishness or sin, rule our lives.

We also show our gratitude to God by our worship. We try to bring the very best to God when we pray alone or with others. Our prayers are real, our singing is strong, and even our church buildings are as beautiful as we can make them.

All of these ways of showing love take a certain amount of strength. It's easy to take others for granted, no matter how much we love them. It's easy to get busy with our own lives and forget to say "thank you." Taking time to show love in a special way takes fortitude.

Considering the way we live today, we would think that most people living a thousand years ago were very poor. But they were grateful to God for what they had, and they wanted to show it. For about four hundred years, in this period that we call the Middle Ages, communities worked together to create amazing buildings that showed how amazing they believed God was. These buildings are called cathedrals, and when you look at them and hear how they were made, you understand what fortitude is.

Now, the word *cathedral* doesn't really describe a style of building; it describes the function or purpose of the building. The main city in every diocese in the Catholic Church has a church building called a cathedral. It's the main church of the diocese, and it's the church of that diocese's bishop. The word *cathedral,* in fact, comes from a Latin word, *cathedra,* which means "chair." A cathedral is the church where the bishop's chair is located, the place where the bishop conducts most of his teaching and leadership. Do you know where the cathedral in your diocese is?

Now, all cathedrals are beautiful in their own way, but the cathedrals that were built in Europe in the Middle Ages were especially wonderful and amazing. They were huge—a football field could fit inside many of them, and their towers could be over three hundred feet tall! They were filled with stained glass and gorgeous art. When you see one of these cathedrals, you have no doubt that the people who built them loved God very much. You also have to wonder: How in the world did they do it?

It's a great question. There were no engines of any kind a thousand years ago. There was no electricity. There were no bulldozers to dig the foundations, no jackhammers to quarry the stone, no trucks to haul the stone from the quarry to the building site, no cranes to lift the stones up hundreds of feet to the top of the cathedrals, and no computers to help design these intricate, complicated buildings. Again, you've just got to wonder. How did they do it?

It took many kinds of workers to build a cathedral, and it took them a long time. Some cathedrals took more than a hundred years to build, and none took fewer than twenty.

The cathedrals were made mostly of stone, with wood supporting the stone in places, and stone, wood, and glass were used for decoration. So, you needed people to cut the stone in the quarries, people to shape the stone into blocks, people to put stone upon stone with mortar in between. You needed wood cutters and carvers. You needed stone carvers, too. You needed blacksmiths to work the metal for doors and other parts of the cathedral. And you needed glassworkers who could make magically beautiful stained-glass windows.

You're probably wondering how huge, heavy stones could be hauled from the country into the city where the cathedral was to be built, and how, then, they could be hauled up to great heights. They didn't have electric motors or steam-powered engines.

True, but they did have their own kind of machines. Their machines—mostly pulleys and levers—were powered by human beings and by animals. You've probably seen hamsters and gerbils running around those little wheels people put in their cages. Well, one of the machines cathedral builders used was similar—only a lot bigger and with people, not hamsters, inside. This "people wheel" was used as a crane to lift heavy stones and other objects high into the air so that they could be placed on the top of high walls or in the towers. How did it work? A couple of lucky workers would run inside the wheel, which was attached to a rope and some other machinery. The rope would then be attached to whatever needed to be lifted, say a stone. The action of the turning wheel would pull on the rope, lifting the stone where it needed to be placed.

And you thought mowing the lawn was tiring!

Cathedrals were built as tall as possible for a reason. The people who built them wanted to draw your eyes upward as you came to Mass or just entered to pray. They wanted the space in the cathedral to remind you of what heaven might be like.

Art filled every corner of a cathedral. Stonework on the inside and outside was carved to tell Bible stories or represent famous people. Many cathedral architects and engineers found a way to get their own faces carved somewhere into a crowd scene, you can be sure.

Most people who worshiped in cathedrals couldn't read. For them, the art and design of the cathedral was like a catechism, or religion book. They could learn about Bible stories in the stone carvings, statues, and stained glass. They could learn about saints that way, too. Going into a cathedral was a wonderful way to learn about God and his love.

Because a cathedral was so big and expensive, an entire community had to be involved in its building, which meant that an entire community had something to be very proud of when it was finished.

Building the cathedral was a difficult and lengthy job. It took a lot of strength from individuals and whole towns. But really, when you think about it, a cathedral is a perfect example of the virtue of fortitude: staying strong through difficult times because you know that what you're doing is for God.

And when you're giving a gift to someone you love, nothing is too hard, because love is always worth an extra dose of fortitude, isn't it?

St. Maria Goretti

Heroes Are Strong Enough to Forgive

You've never been so mad in your life. That report on the history of the Alamo is due tomorrow, and your computer has some weird, incurable disease, so you can't type and you can't do that last bit of research you really need to do.

So when you got home from school, you called your dad for help. You told him what happened and that you really, really needed him to come home early so you could go to the library and finish it up. He promised he'd get home as soon as he could.

And here it is, eight o'clock, the library's closed, and he just got home. You don't really care about his explanations—traffic jams, last-minute phone calls—all you know is that you might just have a really, really bad grade in your future, and it's all his fault.

Forgive? Hah.

Staying mad is, as you probably know, a lot easier than forgiving. Forgiving a person who's hurt you, intentionally or not, takes a lot of strength. It takes that old virtue of fortitude.

But if we listen to Jesus, we find out that when our friendship with Jesus comes first in life, we don't really have a choice about forgiving. "If the same person sins against you seven times a day, and turns back to you seven times and says, 'I repent,' you must forgive" (Luke 17:4).

So how can we do it? How can we find the strength? How can we build up that virtue of fortitude in our lives? Well, we can first start listening to stories of people who have forgiven others, and the story of St. Maria Goretti is full of people like that.

Maria Goretti was born into a poor Italian family in 1890. By 1900, her family had moved from the mountainous northern part of Italy farther south to some farmland around Rome. There, Maria's father agreed to work for a wealthy landowner in return for some land on which to farm his own crops.

Maria was, according to what her friends and family said about her later, a very good girl. She was kind. She was very interested in being close friends with Jesus. She couldn't read or write, but she listened to the Bible stories that her mother told her and she spent a lot of time in prayer, especially for a little girl.

Not long after Maria's family moved to their new home, hard times got even harder. Maria's father got very sick. He suffered for several months, getting weaker and weaker all the time. But, of course, the crops don't care if the farmer is sick or not, and in order to keep up with the work, Maria's father agreed to bring another man and his son into their home to help. The son was around eighteen years old, and his name was Alessandro.

Sadly, Maria's father died in 1900. Maria's mother, Assunta, was left with many children to feed and farmland to work. She really needed the help of Alessandro and his father, which was too bad, because Alessandro was becoming a troublemaker.

He treated others roughly. He went to church sometimes, but in his time alone, he looked at bad books and pictures. He was getting meaner and meaner, and he was also getting more interested in little Maria.

For months, Alessandro tried to get close to Maria. He wanted her to do things with him that she knew were wrong. Of course, Maria said no, over and over. She wanted to keep herself—and Alessandro—from doing wrong.

One day, Alessandro was out in the fields, working with Maria's mother. He asked Assunta to take over the machinery for him for a little while. She agreed. Little did she know what would be happening to her own daughter during that time.

Alessandro returned to Maria's home, where she was sewing and taking care of her sister. He told her to come into a bedroom. She refused, so he forced her to go. He demanded that she let him do things to her that were wrong. Again, she refused. In a rage, Alessandro took out a knife and started stabbing Maria over and over.

At one point, he thought she was dead, so he started to leave the room. She groaned, and so Alessandro came back and stabbed her some more. He stabbed her fourteen times in all.

When the scene was discovered, Maria was rushed to the hospital, but it was too late. The doctors knew she was going to die, so they brought in a priest to prepare her. Although she was in pain, Maria was at peace—her friendship with Jesus had made her strong. It had made her so strong she was even able to do something amazing before she died.

The priest asked her if she could find it in her heart to forgive Alessandro. There was a crucifix in her room, and Maria looked at Jesus suffering there, Jesus who had forgiven those who had killed him. She said yes. "I, too, pardon him. I, too, wish that he could come some day and join me in heaven."

And Maria died, on July 6, 1902.

But the story of the strength to forgive doesn't end there. Alessandro was arrested, tried, and sentenced to thirty years in prison for what he had done. For the first few years, he continued his mean ways and never acted sorry for what he'd done.

Then one day, a bishop came to visit him and asked him if he was sorry. He hadn't been, but he wasn't so sure anymore. That night he had a dream.

In that dream, Maria appeared to him, holding an armful of lilies. She handed them to him, one by one. Alessandro finally understood the evil of what he had done and, even more, understood that he had been forgiven.

From that day on, Alessandro behaved so well in prison that his sentence was cut short by a few years. When he was released, the first thing he did was to travel to visit someone important: Maria Goretti's mother.

He wanted to ask for her forgiveness. It seems impossible and unimaginable that he would receive it. But Assunta Goretti, who had been close to Jesus her whole life, knew what Jesus would have to say about this. She knew that goodness can only flow from goodness. As hard as it was, Assunta found the strength to say yes. She would forgive the man who killed her daughter.

Soon after, the people of the town were shocked to see Maria Goretti's mother and Maria's murderer attending Christmas Mass side by side.

Forgiveness is definitely hard. If it were easy, Jesus wouldn't have to remind us over and over to do it, no matter how many times we've been wronged. Forgiving doesn't mean saying that what happened was okay or wasn't a sin. It doesn't mean saying that it didn't hurt. It means that when someone asks our forgiveness, we need to have the fortitude to see with the eyes of Jesus, our best friend.

Having the strength to forgive means saying yes to peace.

Venerable Cardinal Nguyen Van Thuan

A Hero Never Loses Hope

It's easy to believe God loves you when things are going great. It gets a little harder when times get hard.

When you're doing fine in school, everyone is getting along at home, and you and your friends are having good times, you never really doubt that God's around and that he loves you.

But when disaster strikes, sometimes you wonder. When someone you love suffers, it's natural to wonder where God's love is. When all your plans collapse and no one seems to want you

around, you may wonder why you're here. When you see bad people having good times and being successful, you might be tempted to wonder if loving God is worth the trouble.

During those times, it takes real strength not to turn from God's friendship. It takes fortitude to keep God first and not give in to sadness.

Jesus knew this, of course. He knew how hard it would be. That's why he tells us, over and over, to remember that he's with us always and that we can always talk to him through prayer. That's why he reminds us that no matter how bad things seem, God and his goodness, love, and truth will always win in the end.

Building on that kind of fortitude in your life is really important when you're friends with Jesus. There are lots of stories about real people who have survived terrible ordeals through being strong in the hope of God's love. One of the most powerful stories is that of Venerable Cardinal Nguyen Van Thuan.

Cardinal Thuan, who died in 2002, was born in Vietnam, an Asian country south of China. Catholicism had been brought to Vietnam in the 1500s, but spread more rapidly in the 1800s when France conquered Vietnam. There is a very strong history of the Catholic faith among the Vietnamese, and there are many martyrs, including some in Cardinal Thuan's own family.

Of course, he wasn't born a cardinal—he was just Nguyen Van Thuan when he was born in 1928. Religion was very important to his parents, and his mother read him Bible stories and stories of saints' lives every night. Early in his teen years, Thuan decided he wanted to become a priest.

He studied in Vietnam and in Rome. After he was ordained a priest, Thuan was very busy with his ministry in Vietnam—and very good at it. He was named a bishop at only thirty-eight years of age!

His years as bishop were busy and happy, despite the fact that during those years, war was brewing in his country. The northern part of Vietnam had been taken over by Communists, who believe in a form of government that denies people all kinds of freedoms, including the freedom of religion. Thuan lived in the southern part of Vietnam, and during the 1960s, while he was bishop, the war between the south and the north got more serious—so serious that even the United States got involved.

In 1973, the war ended. South Vietnam had surrendered, the United States withdrew its troops, and the Communist North Vietnamese took over the whole country. One of most important things they wanted to do was to make it impossible for people to follow any kind of religion.

In 1975, the pope gave Thuan a very important job. Thuan was made the archbishop of Saigon, which was the capital of South Vietnam. The government didn't like this at all. They knew how popular Thuan was and what a wonderful leader he was for Vietnamese Catholics. So almost as soon as he was named a bishop, the government arrested him.

First they put him under house arrest in his own home. He couldn't say Mass publicly or even appear in public. During this time, Thuan was tempted to be very sad. He'd been a busy bishop, always organizing groups and meeting people. He couldn't do that anymore. How could he follow God if he couldn't say Mass?

Digging deep, Thuan found strength. He listened to Jesus in prayer. Jesus told him to remember that God was still in charge, and even though things had changed, there was still a way for Thuan to serve.

So, in secret, Thuan asked a little boy who came around the house to help to have his mother buy him some paper. The next night, the boy returned with the paper, and Thuan started to write. He wrote beautiful meditations about hope in God. Every night the boy would take a few pages to his own home, where his own brothers and sisters would make copies. From there, the pages were shared with others. The pages were eventually taken out of the country, where they were published as a book.

Soon, the government decided that house arrest wasn't enough for Archbishop Thuan. They wanted to get him as far away from his people has possible. So they put him on a boat with fifteen hundred other prisoners and sent him to a camp in the north.

Thuan spent thirteen years in prison, nine of them in solitary confinement—alone in a cell, with just two guards outside for company. They were terrible years. The government didn't just imprison Thuan. They forced him and the other prisoners to listen to lectures day after day, telling them how to think. It took a lot of fortitude to live through this and keep faith in Jesus.

There were so many challenges. Can you imagine being all alone in a dirty, tiny cell for nine years? How would you stay sane? How would you keep your faith?

Thuan knew that the challenge would be great. He spent hours every day walking back and forth in his cell so much that he would become paralyzed with arthritis. He sang hymns and prayers. He wrote more books on whatever scraps of paper he could find. And believe it or not, he celebrated Mass.

Wherever he was in prison, alone or with others, Thuan celebrated Mass. When he was first arrested, he asked for a little wine to take with him, saying it was medicine for his stomach. Every day for the next thirteen years, Thuan celebrated Mass. When he was living with other prisoners, he celebrated Mass curled up in his cot in the dead of night. Alone, he celebrated it in his cell, using three drops of wine and one drop of water in the palm of his hand to consecrate into the Blood of Christ. He used bits of bread that he could find to consecrate into the Body of Christ. He kept the Body of Christ in a matchbox in his shirt pocket so that when he saw other Catholic prisoners, he could share Jesus with them.

He later said these were the most beautiful Masses he had ever celebrated in his life.

He carved a cross out of two pieces of wood and hid it in a bar of soap. He made a chain out of electrical wire. When Thuan was finally released from prison in 1988 and then sent out of Vietnam forever in 1991, it was this cross on this chain that he would wear for the rest of his life.

When Archbishop Thuan was arrested, he had a choice to make. He could give in to despair and forget God's love, or he could carry that love with him. It took much fortitude to make the right choice, but he did.

In his darkest days, this is where he found the strength. He remembered that no matter what happened or where he was,

God was still with him. No, he didn't have the busy schedule of a bishop, with lots of groups to meet with and Mass to say before hundreds of people. But he had his fellow prisoners. He had the guards. He had everyone he met, all in need of God's love. He had nothing left but every moment of every day. He would make the choice to fill those moments with God's love.

On the day of his arrest, he wrote: "I will not wait, I will live the present moment, filling to the brim with love. . . . The road of hope is paved with small steps of hope. The life of hope is made of brief minutes of hope. . . . Every minute I want to tell you: Jesus, I love you."

It was there, in that love, that Venerable Cardinal Nguyen Van Thuan found strength. He found the fortitude to be at peace. He found the fortitude to share the love of Jesus with everyone, no matter what they did to him, no matter how badly he felt.

He knew he wasn't alone. And he found the strength to remember and to live in hope, even in the darkest nights, alone in a cell, never knowing what would happen next.

None of us know what will happen tomorrow in our lives. We don't know how our life might change or what surprises—good and bad—might be in store. But remembering that God is with us in every one of those moments gives us the strength to go on with peace in our hearts, ready to love!

Justice

For the Lord is a God of justice.

Isaiah 30:18

Jesus Rises from the Dead

Have you ever said, "It's not fair!" Have you ever thought it?

It just doesn't seem fair that some people have great health and others are sick all the time. It doesn't seem fair that the person who misbehaves in class all the time never gets caught, but you've been silent since September and you just got a detention for asking to borrow a pencil.

Moving beyond your own little world, when you read the news, there's just so much that doesn't seem fair, either. People in poor countries who don't have enough food get their lives swept away in hurricanes. Little children go hungry and are orphaned because their leaders go to war. You could go on and on and on. There is just so much unfairness in the world.

It's enough to make you wonder if God knows what's going on.

Don't worry, he does. And when we're friends with God, as hard as it is sometimes, we can see that he's in charge and that as wrong as things seem now, God will make sure everything is made right in the end—and maybe you and I have a role in helping him make it right.

God has a vision for creation. All things were created good, and he created people to live in harmony with him, with creation, and with each other. Sin has ruined that original vision. When we love God, we're committed to working with God to re-create that original vision of harmony.

When we live that way, we're practicing the virtue called justice. A just person treats others fairly, as God intended them to be treated. A just person treats creation with care, as God wants us to. A just person is willing to do this because he or she trusts that no matter how unfair the world seems, God's vision of justice is worth working for.

What's more, God doesn't just promise us justice in words. He shows us that it will happen. He shows us by raising Jesus from the dead.

Think about it. Is there anything really any more unfair than Jesus' death? He did nothing wrong. He was a completely innocent man, but he was executed as a criminal. Further, we know that death came into our world because of sin. Jesus didn't sin. Why should he have accepted death?

When you look at the innocent Jesus suffering on the cross, it all seems very unfair and very unjust. Until you know the rest of the story, of course.

The rest of the story happens three days after that terrible afternoon on Golgotha. Jesus' body had been cleaned, wrapped in linens, and laid in a tomb carved into a rock. A huge, heavy stone had been rolled across the entrance, and Roman guards had been posted there to make sure no one stole his body.

Early on Sunday morning, some women came to Jesus' tomb. The four Gospels all tell different parts of this story, but it all comes down to this single amazing fact: Jesus' body was gone. The stone had been rolled away, and the tomb was empty.

You can imagine the women's surprise and fear. Someone had stolen Jesus' body. Was his terrible death not bad enough? Why did someone have to do such a thing?

Of course, they soon learned differently. Messengers from God gave them amazing news: Jesus had been raised from the dead, just as he said would happen. They were to go let the disciples know.

So they did, although, not surprisingly, the apostles didn't believe them at first and had to run and see for themselves. What the women had told them was true, and soon they learned this with their own eyes, as Jesus himself came back to them, bringing them peace and even sharing meals!

We don't know exactly how much time Jesus spent with the apostles before he ascended into heaven, but it was enough time for them to learn that everything Jesus had said and done during his life was true. He did, indeed, speak and act with God's authority. He did have new, everlasting life to share with them. God's justice had been done.

It all came down to this: The world had been wrecked by sin. Jesus, through his death and resurrection had fixed the world. God showed us through Jesus that no matter how terrible things were, God would set things right in the end. The blind would see, the lame would walk, and the dead would be raised. Through Jesus, God had opened the door and let us see what the new earth—the earth as he wanted it to be from the beginning—could and would be like. It would be a world of peace, love, and justice.

Life can seem really unfair sometimes, but bringing the virtue of justice into our lives does two things. First, when we remember how Jesus, unjustly executed, was raised from the dead, we can see that what is wrong now will eventually be made right by God. We can trust him on that.

Second, we can see how important it is to let our own choices be guided by God's justice. We don't want to be unfair to others. We want to treat others in a way that brings everyone what they deserve: the love and peace that God wants them to enjoy.

We want to live in the light of God's justice and share it with others. With the risen Jesus in our hearts helping us—we can!

THE FIRST DEACONS

Heroes Bring Justice for the Poor

We say our prayers. We go to Mass. We read the Bible sometimes. We're all trying to follow Jesus in our own lives, as part of our family and as members of churches and schools. Isn't doing all of that enough? What more could there be?

Let's see what Jesus has to say about that:

> "For I was hungry and you gave me food, I was thirsty and you gave me something to drink, I was a stranger and you welcomed me, I was naked and you gave me

> clothing, I was sick and you took care of me, I was in prison and you visited me." Then the righteous will answer him, "Lord, when was it that we saw you hungry and gave you food, or thirsty and gave you something to drink? And when was it that we saw you a stranger and welcomed you, or naked and gave you clothing? And when was it that we saw you sick or in prison and visited you?" And the king will answer them, "Truly I tell you, just as you did it to one of the least of these who are members of my family, you did it to me." (Matthew 25:35–40)

Oh. Maybe there's a bit more to this following Jesus stuff than we thought.

When God looks at us, he sees his children. He sees us living in a world that is broken by sin, a world that isn't the way it's supposed to be. So through grace and friendship with him, God gives us the strength to work with him and make things right. He gives us the chance to practice the virtue of justice.

The earliest Christians knew this very well. The Bible tells us that the first Christians in Jerusalem took care of each other. If someone didn't have enough food, they shared. No one went hungry or without clothes. They took special care of those people who were least able to help themselves.

In those days, those in the most need of help were orphans and widows. You can understand why orphans would need so much help, but you may not see why widows were set apart as people with special needs. If a woman's husband died, couldn't she just go out and get a job?

Well, no. During the time of Jesus, women had very few rights. If her husband died and left behind a business, a widow might be able to keep it and make a living, but that wasn't guaranteed. And if her husband was a laborer who made his living working with his hands wherever he could find a job, well, if he died, he left behind nothing. A widow might be able to pick up some work here and there, but for the most part, she was left poor, especially if she had children to feed and no family of her own left to help her.

So that's why you hear "widows and orphans" spoken of frequently in the Bible—in both the Old and New Testaments—as people who were in special need of help from the community. A community would be judged by God, it was believed, in part by how it cared for the most helpless among them. So caring for widows and orphans was very important to the early Christians.

But the early Christians were busy with other things, too, weren't they? They were a brand-new religion with lots of possibilities and even a few problems. The apostles wanted to tell as many people as possible about Jesus. They were always facing new questions about their faith in Jesus, such as did Christians also have to be Jewish and obey the Jewish Law? And the apostles were facing challenges from religious and government leaders.

How could they do it all? How could the apostles keep on preaching the Good News to as many people as possible, but at the same time take care of the needy among them?

How do you solve a problem like this in your family or school? You know that something needs to be done, but lots of people have lots of other things to do, too. What do you do? You share the responsibility.

And this is what the apostles did. They very much wanted to take care of all those in need in their communities, but they needed to be out and about preaching the gospel. So, as the Acts of the Apostles tells us, they picked some people and gave them a special job.

> And the twelve called together the whole community of the disciples and said, "It is not right that we should neglect the word of God in order to wait on tables. Therefore, friends, select from among yourselves seven men of good standing, full of the Spirit and of wisdom, whom we may appoint to this task, while we, for our part, will devote ourselves to prayer and to serving the word." What they said pleased the whole community, and they chose Stephen, a man full of faith and the Holy Spirit, together with Philip, Prochorus, Nicanor, Timon, Parmenas, and Nicolaus, a proselyte of Antioch. They had these men stand before the apostles, who prayed and laid their hands on them. (Acts 6:2–6)

The apostles were close friends with Jesus. They knew how he cared for the poor. They knew that he preached about the kingdom of God and wanted them to preach about it, too. More than that, they knew that Jesus wanted them to bring the kingdom of God to life in this world as much as possible. That means bringing God's justice into the world. And if they had to do something different and new to get this done, that's just what it would take.

The men they chose were called deacons. These deacons were in charge of helping the poor who were part of the Christian family, and even those who were not Christian. They visited the sick and were in charge of collecting food and money, and of giving it to those in need. It was a very special and important job. One of the deacons—Stephen—was the first person to die for the Christian faith.

No, you can't do everything. You can't save the world all by yourself. But, as the apostles show us, being friends with Jesus means loving others as he does and bringing God's vision of justice into their lives. Begin with prayer. Praying helps us listen with the ears of Jesus and see with his eyes. When we see and hear that way, we learn how much people need help.

And we find a way to bring it to them!

St. Ambrose and Emperor Theodosius

A Hero Stands Up for Fairness

Who does that kid think he is, anyway? Why does he think that he can get away with handing in papers late and leaving class whenever he feels like it to get a drink? No one else can get away with any of that, not for a second. Of course, no one else is the principal's son, either. How unfair!

Unfairness bugs you, and it should. Rules are rules, and just because you happen to be related to someone in charge doesn't mean you shouldn't have to live by the same rules as everyone else.

We should pay attention to the times that we've been unfair, too. Helping a friend lie to her parents is unjust. Her parents deserve the truth just as much as anyone. Not giving someone a chance to write for the school newspaper just because he gets on your nerves is really unjust—that kid deserves a chance just as much as your best friend does.

Being friends with Jesus means that we treat all people the way he treated them—with fairness and justice.

Some people have to learn this the hard way. You probably won't be surprised to learn that some of the most stubborn learners have been powerful leaders. Fortunately, most of the time, right alongside those powerful people have been other people who put friendship with Jesus first and who can point out when God's justice has been forgotten.

In the fourth century, the Roman Empire was led by a man named Theodosius. In some ways, Theodosius was good news for Christians. You may remember that during the first few hundred years after Jesus' death and resurrection, Christians were often persecuted by the Roman Empire. It was illegal to practice Christianity for much of that time, and Christians suffered a great deal for their friendship with Jesus.

A few years before Theodosius came to power, things had begun to change for Christians, and for the better. In 312, an emperor named Constantine had an amazing experience before a battle: He had a dream in which he saw a cross and heard a voice telling him, in Latin, "Under this sign, you will conquer." The story goes that Constantine then had a cross, or perhaps the first two letters of "Christ," put on all of his soldiers' shields, and then went on to win an impossible battle.

Because of this and because of the influence of Christians in his family, especially his mother, St. Helena, Constantine ended the persecution of Christianity in the Roman Empire. He himself did not become a Christian until he was baptized on his deathbed, but under his rule, after three hundred years of persecution, Christians finally had the freedom to worship God publicly, rather than in the underground tombs, caves, and outdoor fields that they had been forced to use before that.

Theodosius became the emperor, years later, in 379. A year after that, Theodosius was baptized as a Christian and soon gave the Christian Church even more rights than Constantine had. In some ways, the news was good for Christians under Theodosius.

But Theodosius was still an emperor and still a man. He still placed a lot of his faith in his own power. We can see how much faith he put in his own power in a terrible incident that happened in a city called Thessalonica in the year 390.

Thessalonica is in the country we now call Greece, but it was then a part of the Roman Empire. The name might be familiar to you because in the first century, St. Paul wrote two letters to the Christians in that city: the First and Second Letters to the Thessalonians.

Theodosius was not concerned with the Christians in Thessalonica, though. He was concerned with the rioters. Crowds had gathered in Thessalonica, unsatisfied with certain ways their city was being ruled. Things got so bad many people in the city started rioting, and in the end, one of Theodosius's trusted senior officials was killed.

This enraged Theodosius, and in his anger, he hatched the most terrible plan of revenge. He had it announced throughout the city that there would be a special show in the city's amphitheater—the outdoor arena that every Roman city had. This was common in those days. You may remember that years before, crowds had gathered in amphitheaters throughout the empire to see not only chariot races and circuses, but also Christians being tortured to death.

The people of Thessalonica had no idea what was awaiting them in this show, but since it was free and because the emperor had told them to come, they filled the seats of the amphitheater to wait for the excitement.

The doors and gates were locked. The emperor's soldiers spread throughout the crowd. And at a signal, they went to work.

In revenge for the riots and the death of one Roman official, all those in the amphitheater were slaughtered by the soldiers. Men, women, and children, young and old, healthy and sick. Theodosius had gotten his revenge. Seven thousand people were murdered by his order.

The news of the massacre spread. Eventually the news reached the city of Milan, in northern Italy, the home of the most well-known and beloved bishop in Italy—Ambrose of Milan.

Bishop Ambrose was, of course, enraged. Seven thousand of God's children had been killed at the word of one man. Theodosius, although he was a baptized Christian, obviously didn't understand his place in the world. He might have had a lot of earthly power, but his power did not extend to deciding who would live and die in this way. Theodosius had decided that God's rules of justice, which tell us "thou shalt not kill" did not apply to him.

Ambrose knew he had to tell Theodosius that he was badly mistaken. God's rules did apply to him, and he would have to pay a price for forgetting that and causing so much suffering.

So Ambrose told the most powerful man in the world that he was not to set foot in a church for a long time. He was not to receive communion. Because of his great sin, he had shut himself off from God and shut himself off from the church.

Ambrose told Theodosius to stay away, pray, and do serious penance to show how sorry he was for what he had done. In those days, people who had committed serious public sins had to do penance in a public way. They had to dress very simply, perhaps even wear clothing made from rough sacks. They had to wear ashes on their foreheads. And of course, they could not set foot in a church.

Amazingly, this is what Theodosius did. Nothing could bring back all those lives he was responsible for murdering, but history tells us that through the strength of Ambrose, Theodosius was at least able to see that what he had done was a great sin and very unjust.

St. Ambrose knew that if the emperor could have seven thousand people killed, it would be very easy for him to add one bishop to that list. But that didn't stop him. Ambrose knew what kind of world God had created and how he wanted his friends to help rebuild that world of peace. Theodosius had been very unjust. To let him just go on and think he had done right would have been unjust, too. Ambrose was dedicated to the virtue of justice, and so in whatever way he could, the emperor had to do something to make up for what he had done.

None of us have committed such a terrible sin as Theodosius did, but there are times that all of us are tempted to treat others unfairly, and there are times when we witness the unfair treatment of others. We are all tempted to try to get around God's rules, given to us in love. We are all tempted to think that God's rules don't apply to us—especially when we plan on treating someone unfairly.

At those moments, we could all use a St. Ambrose in our lives.

The Jesuit Reductions

Heroes Offer Safety

There aren't too many things harder to explain than a bully. Think about it. Imagine your favorite neighborhood bully. It could be a boy or a girl. Bullies come in all sizes and shapes, and use all kinds of force to get their way. They use punches and pinches, but they also use insults and gossip.

Bullying is bad news, no matter how it happens, and bullies need to be stopped. We can also agree that we need to stand up for ourselves when we're bullied, and we need to help others who are being bullied.

It's only right. It's only just. No one deserves to be treated badly by a bully.

Protecting the weak has always been an important part of the church's work. In times when kings and princes used the poor for workers without any concern for their health or welfare, it was the church that tended to the sick and the orphaned.

During the sixteenth and seventeenth centuries, Europeans came over to the New World in droves. They came for all kinds of reasons. Some came because they were curious and interested to see what and who was here. Others came because they were greedy for land and wealth. Others just came for adventure.

The Spanish and Portuguese who arrived in what is now Latin America came for all of those reasons. The Europeans brought much that was good to the New World. They came with violence, it is true, but the indigenous peoples who lived here had violence and war among themselves before the Europeans arrived.

However, although the Europeans brought some good and the indigenous peoples were not perfect themselves, we also can't deny that the Europeans brought much hardship with them. They were not interested in treating the indigenous peoples like human beings. They were not interested in negotiating with them for land or work. They saw the indigenous peoples as little more than animals and treated them that way. They claimed the land for themselves and forced the indigenous peoples to work it for the Europeans' profit. The indigenous peoples suffered greatly.

It is the definition of injustice, isn't it?

Someone needed to stand up for the indigenous peoples. As we have seen time and time again, just about the only people to stand up for the poor when they are being bullied are faithful Christians—and in this case it was priests, nuns, and laypeople who were able to see the indigenous peoples as children of God and deserving of justice.

One of the best examples of this occurred in South America in the seventeenth and eighteenth centuries. In an area that now is made up of the countries of Paraguay, Argentina, Brazil, and Uruguay, indigenous peoples were protected with dignity and care. They were treated with respect and justice by the priests and brothers of the Jesuit order who brought them to live together in mission settlements.

"Jesuit" is another word for a man who is a member of the Society of Jesus, the group of priests and brothers founded by St. Ignatius of Loyola. In the 1600s, the Jesuits had been around for only a few decades, but they had already spread out to every corner of the globe, including South America. There, they saw the suffering of the indigenous peoples at the hands of conquerors, and the Jesuits decided to do something about it. They decided to treat the indigenous peoples with justice; they started mission settlements called reductions.

The reductions were like towns and small cities. Safe behind walls, the indigenous peoples were protected. They were protected from the diseases and bad habits that the Europeans brought with them. They were protected from enslavement by the Europeans. And they were given a chance to learn and prosper.

The Jesuits were in charge of the reductions and made many of the rules, but the indigenous peoples governed themselves. Each year they had elections to choose the leaders in their community. The community leaders met every day after Mass to discuss any problems. All the land in the reduction was owned by the whole community, and the crops produced on the land were shared equally—just as the early Christians shared in Jerusalem.

The indigenous peoples not only grew crops, but they made things as well. They became especially good at making watches and such musical instruments as violins, and their work came to be well-known and valued across the land, and even in Europe.

The Jesuits ran schools in the reductions and taught children—mostly boys, according to the custom of the times—how to read and write in Latin and Spanish. The choirs of the reductions were well known, and the religious celebrations were great, colorful, joyful festivals.

In time, tragedy struck all of the reductions. Some European countries stopped supporting the Jesuits. Spain joined many other countries in making all the Jesuits leave their country and their colonies around the world. This, unfortunately, included the Jesuits who ran the reductions in the Spanish territory of South

America. Some of the reductions were destroyed, and others were given to other religious orders who did not have the same dedication and let them collapse. By 1800, they were all gone.

But in their time, the reductions did much good to protect the indigenous peoples against the Spanish conquerors who would have ended up working them to death. Anytime anyone steps in to protect someone from bad treatment or bullying, you can bet that such goodness is never forgotten and that any time God's justice can shine through is a time worth celebrating.

Blessed Julia Rodzinska and Others

Heroes Rescue Those in Danger

It's hard to imagine how terrifying and horrible it was to be a Jewish person living in Nazi Germany. From 1933, when the Nazi party led by Adolf Hitler took over the government of Germany, to 1945, when the Nazis were defeated at the end of World War II, the German government did its best to get rid of Jewish people wherever it took control.

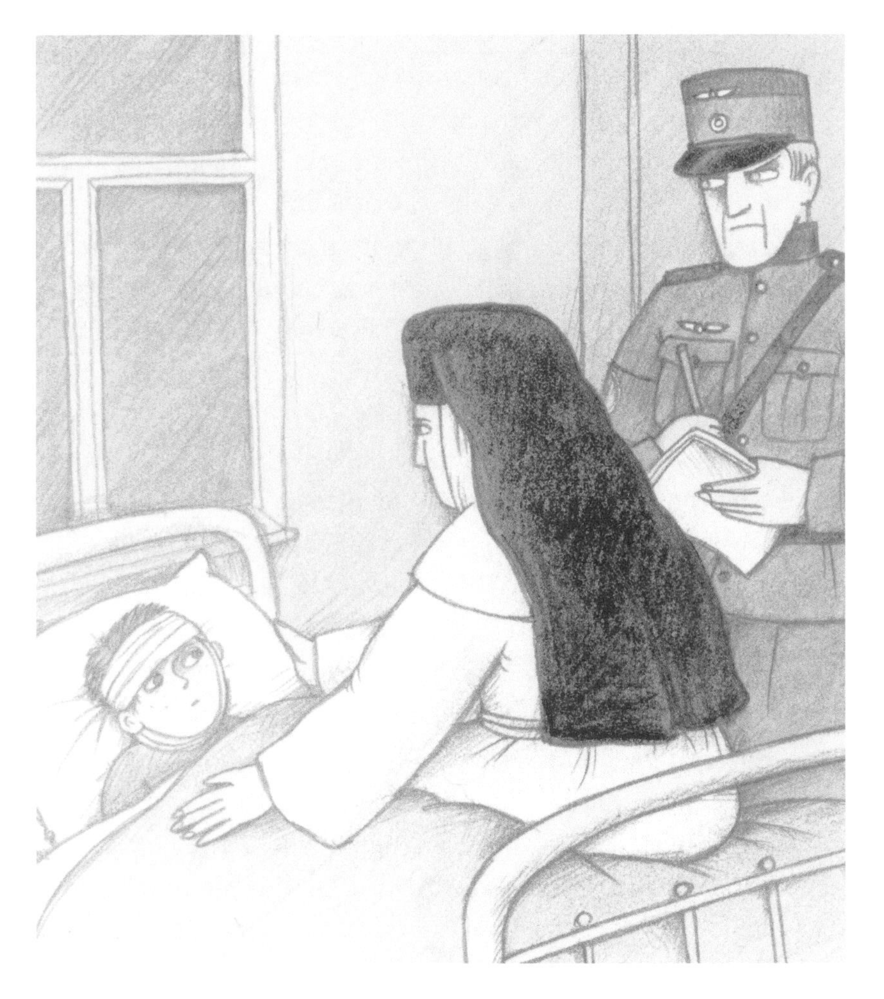

The treatment went from bad to worse. At first, Jewish people lost their jobs and other rights. But by the end of the 1930s, wherever the Nazis ruled, Jews were arrested and sent to concentration camps where they were worked as slaves, used as subjects in medical experiments, and killed.

It was a horrible, unimaginable time. Many people in those Nazi-controlled countries cooperated with the government and turned in their Jewish neighbors to the authorities. But some resisted the Nazis. Throughout Europe, especially in France, Italy, and Poland, ordinary people of all kinds risked their own lives to hide Jews and help them escape to safer countries.

These people are called rescuers. They are true heroes of justice.

Rescuers came from all walks of life. They were individuals who hid other individuals in their homes or barns. In a few cases, whole towns cooperated to save Jewish people. Most famous of all is the French village of Le Chambon–sur–Lignon, a town made up of mostly Protestant Christians, who worked together throughout the whole war to save thousands of Jews from death.

Throughout Europe during these terrible years, many other Christians worked to rescue Jews. Catholic priests, monks, and nuns were in an especially good position to help. They ran big institutions in big buildings: monasteries on many acres of land, schools, hospitals, and orphanages. These were all excellent hiding places!

In Poland, many nuns hid Jewish children in their convents and hospitals. They bandaged the children's faces so they would not be recognized as Jewish by German soldiers. They made out false papers for the children. Some sisters were caught and killed because they were hiding Jewish children. Blessed Julia Rodzinska, Blessed Maria Marta, and Blessed Maria Ewa, among many others, have been recognized by the church for their saintly, heroic work of justice in rescuing Jewish people.

A priest named Fr. Favre was a teacher at a seminary on the border between France and Switzerland. France had been taken over by the Nazis, but Switzerland was a safe country for Jewish people. Fr. Favre saw to it that hundreds of Jewish families were able to sneak around the German border guards to safety in Switzerland. He let Jewish children pretend to be students in his school and Jewish adults pretend to be their visiting parents when the Nazis would come to search. In 1944, Fr. Favre was captured and shot for hiding Jewish people.

There were other ways to work against the Nazis, too. You are used to living in a country where people can say what they want to without the fear of being put in jail. Countries under Nazi rule were not like that. There was no freedom at all. If you spoke against the government and its policies, you would be arrested and possibly killed. Many Catholic leaders refused to be silent about the injustices in Nazi Germany, and they paid the price for speaking the truth.

Blessed Nikolaus Gross had been a mineworker before he joined a political party dedicated to helping workers and speaking out against the Nazis. Even though he worried about how his actions might affect his wife and seven children, he also knew that he had to do what was right. He wrote many articles in his party's newspaper condemning the Nazis, saying that there was no way that anyone who considered themselves Christian could support their policies. He was arrested and sent to a concentration camp where he was killed and his body burned in 1945.

Blessed Titus Brandsma was from the Netherlands. He was a Carmelite brother and a brilliant teacher. He saw what was going on in Germany, and he began to speak against it. He said that Catholic newspapers could not, ever, publish writings that supported Nazi policies. Eventually the Nazis invaded the Netherlands—which was the same country where Anne Frank was hiding when she wrote her diary—and when they did, they wasted no time in arresting Brother Titus. They tried to get him to change his views and to publicly support the Nazis, but, of course, he refused. He knew what was just and what was right.

Eventually, Brother Titus was sent to a concentration camp called Dachau. He worked as a slave along with the other prisoners and was eventually taken to the camp hospital where doctors performed medical experiments on his body. He was poisoned to death in 1942.

There were many, many other rescuers. We know some of their names, and others we don't. During these terrible times, all across Europe men and women of every faith and walk of life, including many Catholic laypeople and religious, stayed strong and decided that they would not let this injustice rule. They would risk their lives for the women, men, and children targeted by Nazis for torture and death. They would hide them and help them escape. They would do what they could to rescue them, no matter the price.

Sometimes learning about sad times like the Holocaust can be very difficult and frightening. It's hard to imagine how people can do such terrible things to each other. But remember that in every sad time you will find heroes. You'll find people who know that God's vision for his world and his beloved children is being ignored. You will find people who refuse to forget that vision and who sometimes give their lives to see that justice—God's justice—still has a place in the world.

Dorothy Day

A Hero Stands for Peace

When we think about all the words, deeds, and promises of Jesus, it sometimes seems too good to be true. Will poor people ever have enough to eat? Will there be peace on earth? Could the world really embrace and live according to the love and justice of God? When we think about how the world would need to change in order for these things to happen, we can lose hope.

But deep in our hearts, we do know those things Jesus promised are possible. (God said they were—with his help, of course.)

And we also know something else. We know that while God plays his part in bringing his word to life in the world, we have a part to play, too.

And that's the part that's hard.

Could we really give up what we need in order to make it happen? Could we live more simply? Could we give more time to other people? Could we forget about our pride and make peace with our enemies?

That's quite a vision. That's quite a set of sacrifices. And look at us—we're so weak, and we're so far from living that vision. We look at our bad habits, we shrug, and we say, "Oh, well. It's too late for me. God can't use me. He only uses perfect people, and I'm sure not perfect."

The lives of holy men and women show us over and over how silly it is to think that way. Every one of the people we have talked about in this book was a weak, limited person just like you. Oh, they did great things, but every one of them had his or her faults, too. Some were stubborn and some had bad tempers. They all had their sins that they confessed to God, just like you do.

Just like you, they were born as limited people into an imperfect family living in a messy world. They all made mistakes along the way. But they kept their eyes on their best friend—Jesus—they grew into holiness, and they were able to live out God's love in amazing ways.

Dorothy Day was one of those holy people. She had a very messy life for a while. But when she really opened her heart to God's love, she was able to turn it around and do great things—great things for the poor and great things in the name of God's justice.

Dorothy was born in New York City in 1897. Her family was happy and busy, and they also moved around a lot. At one point they moved all the way from the East Coast to the West Coast—to Oakland, California. They didn't live there very long, though. When Dorothy was eight years old, there was a terrible earthquake centered in San Francisco, which is across the bay from Oakland, that killed many people and destroyed much of the city. Her family decided it was time to leave before any more disasters struck—and they moved to Chicago.

Believe it or not, the earthquake did bring something good into Dorothy's life. After the earthquake struck, many people were left homeless and food was hard to get. Dorothy's mother jumped in to help without a second thought and spent days helping the victims of the earthquake.

Dorothy carried this memory with her, as well as all of the other memories of her family's kindness and concern for the poor. By the time Dorothy was in college (at the age of only sixteen!), she had decided that helping the poor was about the most important thing any person could do.

Now remember, at this time Dorothy Day was not a Catholic, or even really a Christian. Her ideas of how to help the poor came, not from the examples of the saints, but from the ideas of her time. These ideas—called socialism and communism—suggested that if government was in charge of every part of people's lives, it could see to it that the poor were taken care of and no one was in need.

These seemed like good ideas to Dorothy. She joined groups that believed in these ideas, and she started a career of newspaper writing so that she could share her ideas and the stories of suffering poor people with the world.

Dorothy lived in New York City now, and she led a busy city life. Her friends were writers and artists and people working for change. Life for Dorothy was exciting and busy. She had no real use for faith or friendship with God.

When she was in her late twenties, Dorothy fell in love. She and the man she lived with (they were not married) had a baby together. This baby—named Tamar—changed Dorothy's life, which is what babies have a habit of doing. Dorothy could see something miraculous in her baby's birth. This miracle, she knew, could only come from God.

Dorothy decided to have her baby baptized, and soon after Dorothy became a Catholic herself. Her life was really beginning to change. The man she lived with didn't like her new faith, and he left her. She started to see the problems with her old ways of thinking. Her old friends seemed lost and hurt without God. Their ideas about helping the poor seemed empty, too, without God.

But Dorothy was still interested in justice. She was still moved and saddened by the problems of poor people. Now more than ever, as a friend of Jesus, she knew the importance of putting the poor first in our lives. That's what Jesus did, and that's what we should do, too.

In 1933, Dorothy met a man who would help her bring her ideas together. His name was Peter Maurin. He was from France and was a very unusual man with strong ideas. He encouraged Dorothy to use the gifts God had given her to work for justice for poor people. So he and Dorothy started a group to help. They called it the Catholic Worker.

There were two main parts to Dorothy's Catholic Worker group. First was a newspaper—you remember that Dorothy was a writer, right?—which was "sold" for one cent an issue. The paper contained articles explaining what life for the poor was like and how things could be made better. Dorothy Day wrote a column for every issue of that paper until she died.

The second part of the work of the Catholic Worker were what they called Hospitality Houses. Dorothy believed that Jesus lived in every person who walked on the earth. She believed that we were called to treat the poor as Jesus walking into our lives, in need. So, if we see the face of Jesus in the poor, we don't just give them money and tell them to move on. We don't just pray for them. We don't just set up programs to help them and hope for the best.

No, Dorothy said, we live with the poor, we listen to them, and we make friends with them. In other words, we become poor ourselves. Dorothy remembered God's vision of life for his children: life with no divisions, life lived together in peace. Her work brought that vision of justice to life for many people.

Dorothy Day died in 1980 at the age of eighty-three. During her life she influenced many people. Hospitality Houses were set up across the country and around the world. People came to talk and listen to Dorothy Day, to learn from her.

When they came, this is what they would see: a tall woman dressed in a simple dress, dark stockings, and bulky shoes, often wearing a kerchief of some kind around her head. She was strong and didn't stay silent when something struck her as wrong or unjust.

And most of all, you would have found that Dorothy Day prayed. She prayed to Jesus, Mary, and the saints. She prayed the rosary. She went to Mass every day. She read the Bible and the lives of the saints.

Why did she do all this?

Because Dorothy Day, like all of the people in this book, was best friends with God. She had tried many other ways of living and had tried to put other things first, but in the end, she saw that nothing was more important than God, because there is nothing else we can take with us after we die except God's friendship.

Early in Dorothy's life she cared about helping poor people, but she didn't care about God's friendship. When she had hard times, where did she turn? How would she realize where her desire to help really came from?

God found a way to help her, didn't he?

Dorothy answered the call to live for the poor and to try to help them in their suffering. But the problem is so big—who can ever really help?

God found a way.

Dorothy believed that God wanted a peaceful world, not a world at war. She was against violence of any kind for any reason. Can there ever be such a world?

Dorothy believed that God would find a way.

God made this beautiful earth. He made each of us—his beautiful daughters and sons. Sin may have entered our world and made life hard, but God has given us a great gift to help. He's given us the chance to be friends with him and to build our lives around his love. When we do this, we are working with God to bring love and justice back to life in this world.

When we live this way, we are heroes.

We are heroes of the kingdom of God!

INDEX

Page numbers in bold following the name of a person indicate the beginning of a chapter about that person.

Z